Media Education and the (Re)Production of Culture

Critical Studies in Education and Culture Series

Popular Culture, Schooling and the Language of Everyday Life
Henry A. Giroux and Roger I. Simon

Teachers As Intellectuals: Toward a Critical Pedagogy of Learning
Henry A. Giroux

Women Teaching for Change: Gender, Class and Power
Kathleen Weiler

Between Capitalism and Democracy: Educational Policy
and the Crisis of the Welfare State
Svi Shapiro

Critical Psychology and Pedagogy: Interpretation of the
Personal World
Edmund Sullivan

Pedagogy and the Struggle for Voice: Issues of Language,
Power, and Schooling for Puerto Ricans
Catherine E. Walsh

Learning Work: A Critical Pedagogy of Work Education
Roger I. Simon, Don Dippo, and Arleen Schenke

Cultural Pedagogy: Art/Education/Politics
David Trend

Raising Curtains on Education: Drama as a Site for
Critical Pedagogy
Clar Doyle

Toward a Critical Politics of Teacher Thinking: Mapping
the Postmodern
Joe L. Kincheloe

Building Communities of Difference: Higher Education
in the Twenty-First Century
William G. Tierney

The Problem of Freedom in Postmodern Education
Tomasz Szkudlarek

Education Still under Siege: Second Edition
Stanley Aronowitz and Henry A. Giroux

Media Education and the (Re)Production of Culture

DAVID SHOLLE and STAN DENSKI

Critical Studies in Education and Culture Series
Edited by Henry A. Giroux and Paulo Freire

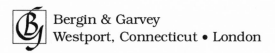

Bergin & Garvey
Westport, Connecticut • London

Library of Congress Cataloging-in-Publication Data

Sholle, David.
    Media education and the (re)production of culture / David Sholle
and Stan Denski.
        p.   cm.—(Critical studies in education and culture series,
ISSN 1064–8615)
    Includes bibliographical references (p.   ) and index.
    ISBN 0–89789–254–2 (alk. paper).—ISBN 0–89789–255–0 (pbk.:
alk. paper)
        1. Audio-visual education—Social aspects—United States.
2. Critical pedagogy—United States.   I. Denski, Stan.   II. Title.
III. Series.
LB1043.S456   1994
371.3'35—dc20   93–40159

British Library Cataloguing in Publication Data is available.

Library of Congress Catalog Card Number: 93–40159
ISBN: 0–89789–254–2
        0–89789–255–0 (pbk.)
ISSN: 1064–8615

First published in 1994

Bergin & Garvey, 88 Post Road West, Westport, CT   06881
An imprint of Greenwood Publishing Group, Inc.

Printed in the United States of America

The paper used in this book complies with the
Permanent Paper Standard issued by the National
Information Standards Organization (Z39.48–1984).

10 9 8 7 6 5 4 3 2 1

Contents

Series Foreword

Within the last decade, the debate over the meaning and purpose of education has occupied the center of political and social life in the United States. Dominated largely by an aggressive and ongoing attempt by various sectors of the Right, including "fundamentalists," nationalists, and political conservatives, the debate over educational policy has been organized around a set of values and practices that take as their paradigmatic model the laws and ideology of the market place and the imperatives of a newly emerging cultural traditionalism. In the first instance, schooling is being redefined through a corporate ideology which stresses the primacy of choice over community, competition over cooperation, and excellence over equity. At stake here is the imperative to organize public schooling around the related practices of competition, reprivatization, standardization, and individualism.

In the second instance, the New Right has waged a cultural war against schools as part of a wider attempt to contest the emergence of new public cultures and social movements that have begun to demand that schools take seriously the imperatives of living in a multiracial and multicultural democracy. The contours of this cultural offensive are evident in the call by the Right for standardized testing, the rejection of multiculturalism, and the development of curricula around what is euphemistically called a "common culture." In this perspective, the notion of a common culture serves as a referent to denounce any attempt by subordinate groups to challenge the narrow ideological and political parameters by which such a culture both defines and expresses itself. It is not too surprising that the theoretical and political distance between defining schools around a common culture and denouncing cultural difference as the enemy of democratic life is relatively short indeed.

This debate is important not simply because it makes visible the role that schools play as sites of political and cultural contestation, but because it is within this debate that the notion of the United States as an open and democratic society is being questioned and redefined. Moreover, this debate provides a challenge to progressive educators both in and outside of the United States to address a number of conditions central to a postmodern world. First, public schools cannot be seen as either objective or neutral. As institutions actively involved in constructing political subjects and presupposing a vision of the future, they must be dealt with in terms that are simultaneously historical, critical, and transformative. Second, the relationship between knowledge and power in schools places undue emphasis on disciplinary structures and on individual achievement as the primary unit of value. Critical educators need a language that emphasizes how social identities are constructed within unequal relations of power in the schools and how schooling can be organized through interdisciplinary approaches to learning and cultural differences that address the dialectical and multifaceted experiences of everyday life. Third, the existing cultural transformation of American society into a multiracial and multicultural society structured in multiple relations of domination demands that we address how schooling can become sites for cultural democracy rather than channeling colonies reproducing new forms of nativism and racism. Finally, critical educators need a new language that takes seriously the relationship between democracy and the establishment of those teaching and learning conditions that enable forms of self and social determination in students and teachers. This suggests not only new forms of self-definition for human agency, it also points to redistributing power within the school and between the school and the larger society.

Critical Studies in Education and Culture is intended as both a critique and as a positive response to these concerns and the debates from which they emerge. Each volume is intended to address the meaning of schooling as a form of cultural politics, and cultural work as a pedagogical practice that serves to deepen and extend the possibilities of democratic public life. Broadly conceived, some central considerations present themselves as defining concerns of the Series. Within the last decade, a number of new theoretical discourses and vocabularies have emerged which challenge the narrow disciplinary boundaries and theoretical parameters that construct the traditional relationship among knowledge, power, and schooling. The emerging discourses of feminism, post-colonialism, literary studies, cultural studies, and post-modernism have broadened our understanding of how schools work as sites of containment and possibility. No longer content to view schools as objective institutions engaged in the transmission of an unproblematic cultural heritage, the new discourses illuminate how schools function as cultural sites actively engaged in the production of not only knowledge but social identities. *Critical Studies in Education and Culture* will attempt to encourage this type of analysis by emphasizing how schools might be addressed as border institutions or sites of crossing actively involved in exploring, reworking, and translating the ways in which culture is produced, negotiated, and rewritten.

Emphasizing the centrality of politics, culture, and power, *Critical Studies in Education and Culture* will deal with pedagogical issues that contribute in novel ways to our understanding of how critical knowledge, democratic values, and social practices can provide a basis for teachers, students, and other cultural workers to redefine their role as engaged and public intellectuals.

As part of a broader attempt to rewrite and refigure the relationship between education and culture, *Critical Studies in Education and Culture* is interested in work that is interdisciplinary, critical, and addresses the emergent discourses on gender, race, sexual preference, class, ethnicity, and technology. In this respect, the Series is dedicated to opening up new discursive and public spaces for critical interventions into schools and other pedagogical sites. To accomplish this, each volume will attempt to rethink the relationship between language and experience, pedagogy and human agency, and ethics and social responsibility as part of a larger project for engaging and deepening the prospects of democratic schooling in a multiracial and multicultural society. Concerns central to this Series include addressing the political economy and deconstruction of visual, aural, and printed texts, issues of difference and multiculturalism, relationships between language and power, pedagogy as a form of cultural politics, and historical memory and the construction of identity and subjectivity.

Critical Studies in Education and Culture is dedicated to publishing studies that move beyond the boundaries of traditional and existing critical discourses. It is concerned with making public schooling a central expression of democratic culture. In doing so it emphasizes works that combine cultural politics, pedagogical criticism, and social analyses with self-reflective tactics that challenge and transform those configurations of power that characterize the existing system of education and other public cultures.

Acknowledgments

We would like to thank Henry Giroux and Peter McLaren for their inspiration and support of this project. A particular thank you goes to David Tetzlaff for significantly contributing to this book through conversations; and through position papers written with David Sholle that were used in the development of chapter 6.

I especially thank Lisa McLaughlin for her invaluable encouragement, criticism and personal support. I dedicate this book to her. Additional thanks are due to Caroline Kaltefleilter for research assistance, Ann Storer, John Higgins, and Barnum & Bailey.

—David Sholle

I would like to thank my father, Michael F. Denski, and my wife, Cheryl for their love and support. And I would like to dedicate this book to Karin Sandell, who showed me the ropes, and to Allen Happe, who showed me that the world was bigger than I thought.

—Stan Denski

Media Education and the (Re)Production of Culture

Introduction

CULTURE, PEDAGOGY, POLITICS

There is an unmistakable irony in watching the United States offer itself as role model to the various projects of democratization unfolding throughout eastern Europe even as the very activities inherent to notions of participatory democracy (e.g., voter turnout, literacy, etc.) continue their steady decline inside our borders. For those striving for social change, there is an experience of tangible depression in witnessing the growing power of neoconservative ideology. The borders and boundaries of this ideological cultural formation are marked by numerous signposts: the renewed attacks upon the hard-won rights of women (in the holy name of morality), racial and ethnic minorities (in the name of a mythological meritocracy), and gays and lesbians (in the timeless name of nature); the steady increase of corporate and state power; the continued melding together of the state, the market and the media, and the corresponding erosion of an ever-diminishing democratic public sphere; the conflation of the corporate and the public into one vague and amorphous collective philosophy of money and nostalgia; and the declamation that recent gains in multicultural education represent little more than the thinly veiled virus of political correctness (which in a twisted Orwellian logic has as its goals the restriction of free discussion and the subversion of a stable and coherent canon of Western culture). Finally in the face of all of this, the political left has been weakened by a spiraling fragmentation and factionalization into a complex yet redundant theoretical melange of suffocating identity politics and reactionary and nihilistic postmodernisms.

These conditions are representative of the environment for theoretical development in the last years of the twentieth century. Under these conditions attention is deflected away from the critical scrutiny of the present historical conjuncture. Instead, the dominant cultural institutions unreflectively celebrate an imagined coherent and homogeneous culture in which difference is positioned as obstinance, an unyielding arrogance in the face of an amiable and innocuous mainstream of naturalized normative values and relations. The educational plans of the Bush administration supported this mainstream in a double-barreled attack that aimed for a return to "universal" values while bolstering U.S. economic advantage. Despite Bush's political demise, this legacy is still with us. Meanwhile, the gains rooted in the civil rights movement in support of citizen education and diversity are being attacked head-on by an amalgam of conservative institutions rooted in think tanks and the popular press. Mary Louise Pratt offers us a powerful image of the insecurity and anxiety often engendered by multicultural, multiethnic and multilingual models of education:

Even among the many people ready for change one seems to hear voices asking "If I give up white supremacy who am I; Am I still American; Am I still white; If I give up homophobia who am I; Am I the same as gay; If I give up misogny am I still a man; a woman; an American; If I learn Spanish does it make me Mexican; What ties me to these gays, these feminists, these Salvadorans, these Vietnamese, these Navaho, these white people?" (1990, 10)

Obscured in the rhetoric of the neoconservative assault is the notion of schools as one remaining site of an ever-diminishing democratic public sphere. Also lost is an earlier understanding of the role of the university as a subversive institution, designed to overturn entrenched attitudes of inhumanity, arrogance and intolerance. As the United States struggles with the uncertain character of its new identity in the transformed world of the next century—in particular its loss of economic superiority and changes in the meaning of military superiority—the neoconservative vision of schools as supply mechanisms designed to meet the needs of an increasingly competitive world marketplace is grounded in the mythology of the "golden years" of post–World War II America.

The most public of the neoconservative critics have attacked multicultural models of education through employing the affective security offered by an ahistorical nostalgia in an era of economic insecurity. The result of this call for an educational fundamentalism—a return to "basic values"—has been to close off that space within public discourse for the discussion of more progressive models of schooling as a means toward the project of a radical and emancipatory democracy. That is, the idea of the development of critical citizens, restoring in the process the subversive character of the contemporary university, has been replaced by the project of a democracy-under-construction in which the function of education is the production of "good" citizens.

Our purpose in drawing this larger portrait is to frame properly the more specific issues of media studies and media education. These are not issues restricted solely to the territory of education but are inherently political and ideological in character. The specific concerns of media curriculum and more general educational issues will always be woven into the histories of gender, race and class conflicts in the United States and elsewhere. Michael Apple argues:

I am even more convinced now that until we take seriously the extent to which education is caught up in the real world of shifting and unequal power relations we will be living in a world divorced from reality. The theories policies and practices involved in education are not technical.They are inherently ethical and political and they ultimately involve—once this is recognized—intensely personal choices about what Marcus Raskin calls "the common good." (1990, viii)

KNOWLEDGE, WEALTH, AND POWER (DAYDREAMS AND THE LONG REVOLUTION)

This is the terrain in which we must locate ourselves, both theoretically and affectively. It is in this context that we must develop that mix of realism and optimism within which the individual and collective energies necessary to accomplish what must be accomplished can even be imagined. It is this mix of struggle and hope, feeling and theory, which describe the cultural process Raymond Williams has called "the long revolution":

I believe that the system of meanings and values which a capitalist society has generated has to be defeated in general and in detail by the most sustained kinds of intellectual and educational work. . . . Anything as deep as a dominant structure of feeling is only changed by active new experience. . . . We have to learn and to teach each other the connections between a political and economic formation, a cultural and educational formation, and perhaps hardest of all the formations of feeling and relationship which are our immediate resources in any struggle. (1989, 76)

In that education is always built upon a vision (at times competing visions) of the future, Henry Giroux (1990) likens the idea of a university education to the notion of daydreaming about democracy. In other words, like the process of daydreaming, the university (and more specifically media education) must be fundamentally involved in the production of images of that which is yet to be. "This is after all what university life should be all about; the politics and ethics of dreaming a better future and dreaming a new world." (117)

Within these territories of politics and education, culture and daydreams, those spaces that open onto issues and questions regarding the mass media represent our point of entry into this debate. Our goal is to develop a cultural politics of media education by building bridges between these disparate and complex interests. It is through the bridging of the theoretical traditions of media studies with those of critical education studies that we hope to offer a cultural politics capable of avoiding the pitfalls of both a hollow rhetoric and a debilitating pessimism. These imagined bridges allow for the possibility of theory's reconnection with practice. An emergent critical media praxis could allow new alternatives to arise from the negotiation between theoretical discourses and those of the cultural (i.e., media and educational) marketplace.

We can begin to lay the groundwork for a more detailed analysis of media education by linking recent conversations in contemporary education to the greater historical transformations of contemporary culture. It is in this sense that the question, "What is contemporary education trying to become?" is linked to the greater question, "What is the United States trying to become?" Our point here is uncomplicated; any effort directed toward meaningful changes in the structure of contemporary media education is by definition directed at greater transformations of existing social relations. And this discourse of transformation is itself inexorably bound up with the current public debate over the future character and purpose of education in general in the United States.

We must approach this greater battle over the social function of education with an initial and explicit awareness that the array of social problems facing the United States is pedagogical as well as political. Power and knowledge, the political and the pedagogical, are caught up in the complex interplay between wealth and imagination. Antecedent to the acquisition of wealth and power is the way we acquire an understanding of what is and is not possible. It is in this manner that social problems involve questions of pedagogy through the interference of politics in the systems and structures through which and in which learning is produced and acquired. In offering a model for schooling as cultural politics, this suggests, on one hand, the theoretical power of a critical theory, of education (a first glimpse of the other side of the bridge) and on the other, a sense of how media (in its production and distribution) and media education (in the professional training approach so common to the contemporary U.S. university) are implicated in the reproduction and maintenance of current asymmetrical conditions of wealth and power, politics and desire.

DISTANCING DICHOTOMIES, SCHIZOPHRENIA AND A PEDAGOGY OF HOPE (TRAVELING THEORY AND THE BUILDING OF BRIDGES)

The contemporary mass media represent both an impenetrably dense nexus of affective alliances, and a complex assemblage of economic structures, distribution networks, production centers and regulatory agencies responsible for the highly organized and controlled flow of both the deeply structured materials of capital and labor and the surface elements of information, entertainment and mild sedation. At any given moment the contemporary mass media are under close scrutiny for trace elements of functions served, gratifications sought, patriarchal imagery, signifier/signified, pastiche, bricolage and so on. At the theoretical level the study of the mass media has always contained a critical component—from early propaganda studies, to the Frankfurt School's account of cultural domination, to the ubiquitous ideological analysis of poststructuralism and neo-Marxism. Ten years ago it seemed that the theoretical territory of a "critical study of the media" was clearly formed: the media needed to be examined through (1) a political economy of media institutions and practices, (2) an analysis of the politics of signification and (3) a historical and theoretical account of the working of hegemony and the resultant "struggle over meaning" (see Gurevitch, et al., 1982). Since that time, cultural studies has shifted the focus to the appropriation of media; that is, it has focused on the struggle with hegemony. However, an emerging popular cultural studies approach has increasingly expanded notions of resistance to hegemony to include such a wide menu of media engagements (of soap opera viewers, slam dancers, Star Trek fans, etc.) as to effectively remove most of the politics from the concept (see Morris, 1988; Sholle, 1991).

The emerging body of theory and method at times loosely collected under the signpost of "cultural studies" has in its Birmingham origins a tradition of positioning itself against the more deterministic strains of critical theory. In the recent literature of cultural studies, however, there is a recurrent pattern of increasing the distance between a given reformulation of critical studies (as audience studies) and its origins in the post-Marxist critical theory of the Frankfurt School. But doing cultural studies does not necessarily entail washing over the first two territories of critical media studies (political economy and ideological analysis). In fact, as Lawrence Grossberg (1992) has noted, cultural studies should map out the complex effects and relations that circulate in and around the cultural. This entails a return to concerns with the contexts of power and the structure of historical agency.

In this context, our concerns are with the ways in which the dominant forms of entertainment media in the United States (television, radio, film, etc.) function as a primary mechanism in the reproduction and maintenance of an array of dominant cultural values. Through the constant flow of images and sound—through the operations of hegemony in support of a dominant ideology[1]—the cultural is continually transformed into the natural, that is, the naturalization and mystification of gender relations, class relations, racial relations and so on. Through this ubiquitous flow of images and sound a "common sense" understanding of the world and the myriad relations within this world is produced, reproduced and maintained. This is not to deny that sites of resistance and struggle exist in opposition to the dominant culture, but the historical context of domination must be broached before one can locate those strategies that produce a resistance that matters.

These concerns extend into further considerations of how undergraduate students are educated in preparation for entering the media industries. In this regard, it is important to understand that in the transatlantic adoption of a tradition of British cultural studies—the work of the Birmingham Centre in particular—the original emphasis of that project upon adult education was somehow lost. While a tradition of critical/cultural analysis of media has been articulated with increasing sophistication throughout the past two decades, the result of this omission is, we believe, quite striking and significant. Absent from the critical discourse surrounding questions of media, society and culture has been what we will describe as a reflexive moment. We want to argue that it is through such a moment that critical analyses of contemporary media might be theoretically connected to the complicit role of the contemporary university in the training of new generations of media students in the increasingly marketable skills and conventions of mediated cultural reproduction. We also believe that this might shed added light upon the failure of left intellectual critics to reach the lay audiences at whom their efforts are ultimately directed.

Our goals in this book are caught up in a metaphor of building bridges. We believe that by bridging media studies and critical pedagogy many of the problems—theoretical and practical—of media and media education might be better addressed. Antecedent to this, however, is the task of repair and maintenance upon the bridges that link media studies to critical theory, and we believe such a repositioning to be an integral component in any effort to redefine and restructure contemporary media education.

This metaphor of bridges is extended into the further image of travel (what is after all the function of a bridge?): metaphorical bridges over which theory might travel. Edward Said's notion of traveling theory, the idea that a theory has no fixed political meaning but takes on different meanings based upon the specific location of its use, raises a number of crucial questions: How do theories travel geographically across disciplines? What are the implications of this theoretical migration? How might such a metatheoretical geography chart the effects upon theory of travel and displacement? And what might these effects be? Travel disorients but does so through rendering the familiar strange, thus offering new perspectives upon old and new alike.

These bridges that we will attempt to initially envision and eventually construct involve a renewed consideration of aspects of our own lives-in-the-world. In particular it seems to us—and we speak from our locations as teachers of media theory and practice—that our lives have become increasingly compartmentalized. As the personal, the professional and the political are shunted into separate spheres, one of the more pressing tasks we face involves the subsequent reintegration of our lives as teachers with our lives as citizens. In that we can never purge the personal, ethical and political from the discourse of curriculum, we must seek strategies which offer us reflexive moments within which we might examine our own subject positions as educators.

Our investment in this project arises out of efforts to address feelings of schizophrenia, feelings shared by many friends and colleagues with professional backgrounds prior to their entry into higher education (Denski, 1991). Our fascination with the practice of media (video, audio, photography, graphics, etc.) led eventually back to the university, often for the initial purposes of skill enhancement and/or career development. The newfound pleasures of instructing others in the techniques and mechanics of design and production and a growing awareness of other advantages offered by the academic environment drew us into graduate programs. It was there where we were introduced to an array of new theoretical perspectives. Marxist critical theory, feminist theory, literary criticism and an overflowing array of ideas offered new ways of examining the complex relations among various cultural forms, the lives of individual and aggregate media consumers and the various sites and struggles for meaning. Eventually, we embarked upon our careers. And our schizophrenia flowered.

The structures of contemporary media education offer the ideal growth medium for our condition. In our research, we used those methods that identify the various ways in which the contemporary entertainment media function to privilege some voices while silencing others. In our teaching—in the undergraduate classroom in particular—we instructed rooms full of future sportscasters, news anchors, music video directors, corporate training filmmakers and the like in all the basics of audio recording, camera movement, editing production design and so on. Media had become a growth industry in undergraduate degree programs. We were asked (and responded with vitae and references) to be teachers of media production and critical media scholars. We were invited to become schizophrenics.

Our condition (part and parcel, perhaps, of the postmodern condition) was brought on and encouraged by a spiraling series of what we will call distancing dichotomies (such as teacher versus student, scholar versus teacher, teaching versus research, research versus production, the theoretical versus the practical, the "real world" versus the "ivory tower"). Through the disruption of these distancing dichotomies, through the reintegration of theory into practice, a critical pedagogy of the media classroom offers a pedagogy of hope. In the collapse of new theory into new practice—into new formulations of the self—a cure for our schizophrenia is offered.

GOALS AND PROMISES, DREAMS AND VISIONS (AN OUTLINE OF FOCUS DIRECTION AND PURPOSE)

Television is the most powerful tool for the reproduction and maintenance of the normative values of dominant culture ever known, ever imagined. In the historical context of postmodern late capitalism the culture industries exhibit the added ability to subsume, diffuse and incorporate into themselves those isolated expressions of difference that represent potential sites of cultural resistance. Bachelor degree programs in media exist, by and large, to train new generations of young people to enter these industries and contribute to this ongoing (and seemingly endless) cycle of production, reproduction, diffusion and containment. In other words, the mass media represent the greatest force for social control ever imagined and media education represents an acritical and celebratory indoctrination into the mechanisms and techniques of this control. What is required to address these conditions is a critical theory of media education encompassing the relationship of media education to media production and the relationship of that production to the reproduction of the asymmetrical relations of power and privilege that define the character of contemporary U.S. culture—a critical sociology of media education examining the various links between media curriculum and the media marketplace.

Postmodern media culture has become a buffer zone, a paradoxical site in which youth lives out a virtually impossible relationship to the future (Grossberg, 1992). This analysis of the media university/industry must also be refracted through the theoretical apparatus of contemporary postmodern theory. Such an analysis should consider the possibility that ripples from the collapse of Jean-François Lyotard's (1984) grand narratives are evident in the collapse of the traditional classifications and categories of liberal education and are particularly visible in the terrain of media education (Ulmer, 1989). We will approach these questions using this image of theory traveling across metaphorical bridges built between media studies and critical pedagogy. The effects of this travel may enable our project to be, in the end, not solely one of critique (sifting through the ashes from the ruins of a project of deconstruction) but of building the world (or at the very least imagining that world) out of the fires of a project of reconstruction.

Part One: Overviews and Foundations

One way of understanding the role played by the contemporary mass media in the greater mechanism of cultural hegemony is see it as equal to the sum total of the various roles played by the men and women who populate the various strata of the media industries. It is their actions in the day-to-day practice of their professional lives that construct the ways in which the mass media contribute to the continued erosion of the kind of democratic public sphere necessary for the very possibility of an emancipatory democracy. Increasingly, undergraduate university media degree programs are participating in producing those individuals who enter and rise to positions of power within the media industries. It is our purpose in this book to extend the critique offered in the literature of critical pedagogy into a specific examination of the conditions of contemporary undergraduate media education in the United States.

A second way of understanding the role of contemporary media is to center on its relations to everyday life—its ubiquitous presence as the source for the iconography of our own and our students' lives. At the undergraduate level, media education has ignored developing a project of media literacy in favor of programs of professional development. This pedagogy separates students' lives into roles of producer and consumer, and is unable to articulate how an understanding of the social, political and cultural effects of the media bear upon the practice of producing media. A critical pedagogy of media would serve to reintegrate our lives, focusing on the political and cultural implications of both watching and producing.

A discontent with present practices gives rise to this book, but this is not offered simply as a negative evaluation. We are also led by hope (in Freire's sense) that a positive project can be developed. This project, then, is conceived as resistant (in Foucault's sense: i.e., as a productive act, an action of transformation). Our goal is the description of a pedagogy of hope, the production of a transformative alternative practice, a course of action that produces against the grain of dominant ideology.

This book is aimed at scholars, writers, researchers and educators working within two distinct metadisciplinary locales: mass media studies (incorporating such divergent areas as film, video, journalism, advertising, and broadcasting) and education (with a particular emphasis upon critical education theory and practice). As our goal throughout is directed at the construction of bridges across these literatures, the first two chapters introduce each audience to the other.

Chapter 1 presents an overview of the literature of critical pedagogy, with attention directed at the works of Paulo Freire, Michelle Fine, Michael Apple, Henry Giroux, Peter McLaren and others. The tradition of critical pedagogy details a crisis in democracy rooted in the structure and character of schooling in the United States. This chapter will explicate the key theoretical concepts in this literature leading toward its more specific application to university media education.

Chapter 2 presents a similar overview of the literature of mass communication theory, paying particular attention to the history of mass media theory in its travels within the American traditions of communication study. We particularly note the manner in which mass communication theory has served as a silencing mechanism, resulting in the separation of that theory from practice. The more recent adoption of cultural studies and other critical approaches to the media offers a means of partially overcoming these problems. However, while contemporary media theory and criticism has offered a complex analysis and deconstruction of the various mass media as cultural forms, it has been the recent tendency of radical theory to spiral downward into an intellectual nihilism, as it has been a tendency of more liberal pluralist efforts to ignore questions of critical/political inquiry in favor of more descriptive and celebratory analyses of popular culture. We believe that the bridging of the theoretical traditions of media studies with critical pedagogy may offer a powerful alternative solution to these conditions.

Part Two: The Structural Problematic of Media Education

In that a cultural politics of education must consider the intellectual, moral and political mission of the university as a cultural and historical institution, so must a cultural politics of media education consider the university's mission in relation to the greater relationship of the mass media to society. Chapter 3 lays the groundwork for the interrogation of the theoretical character of mass communication undergraduate degree programs. This will be developed through the explication of various conditions representative of the current state of media education in the United States. The analysis will attend to the rise in popularity of media-related degree programs, the structure and emphasis of individual programs and the location of these programs within the university structure. Chapter 4 employs the theoretical critique of critical pedagogy in an examination of the tradition of the liberal arts and the specific role of media studies within that tradition. In this manner the process of "problematizing the liberal arts" becomes a subsection of an analysis of media education and the contemporary university. Chapter 5 pinpoints the antecedent pedagogical conditions that constrain the development of a critical media pedagogy within the contemporary university and begins the process of offering a way out. How may the critique presented by critical pedagogy be used to offer solutions leading toward a reconstruction of media studies in higher education in opposition to the complicit role the current pedagogical practice plays in the denigration of an emancipatory democracy? How may these solutions be presented in a manner cognizant of the pragmatic dimensions of the broader conditions of university life?

Part Three: Toward a Critical Media Pedagogy

The final chapters concretize the general suggestions advanced in chapter 5, not in order to offer a cookbook for critical media pedagogy, but rather to suggest specific practices that should be a part of any such democratic form of media pedagogy. Critical pedagogy's critique of the various distancing dichotomies of theory/practice, teaching/research, teacher/scholar, real world/ivory tower are applied to their operations within the specific context of media education. These dichotomies are "distancing" in the manner in which they work to force a separation of the professional, personal and political dimensions of our lives, while also diffusing the resistant potential of difference. As media curricula (in their career-training model) become increasingly specialized, discussions of the underlying theoretical dimensions of media practice (i.e., political, ethical, moral) are inevitably positioned as irrelevant to the concerns of those seeking employment. Theory is, in these conditions, structured as an elite kind of knowledge beyond the interests and abilities of undergraduates. Chapter 6 proposes practices for overcoming these conditions, particularly drawing upon the example of the teaching of television production. Chapter 7 further concretizes the general recommendations of chapter 5 by offering specific suggestions for the development of the overall media studies curriculum.

We thus conclude a movement from the general theoretical overview to the specifics of practice. We offer a range of alternatives representing both ideal conditions and realistic intermediate responses. Ultimately we offer a direction in which to proceed.

NOTE

1. It should be noted that a "dominant ideology" does not necessarily imply a monolithic, singular system of discourse. The "dominant" can function through fragmentation and multiplication, that is, through the multiplication of discourses whose logic is short-circuited and dispersed. But such a fragmentation can still add up to a social and cultural common sense. In fact, in the conditions of late capitalism, the "dominant" most likely functions in such a fragmented manner, working as much by denial as by affirmation. See Eagleton (1991) and Sholle (1988).

Part One:

Overviews and Foundations

Chapter One

The Theoretical Character of Critical Pedagogy

INTRODUCTION

The demise of education in the United States is a given in current political discourse, whether from the right or the left. But, what that demise consists of, how it arose and how to overcome it are hotly contested questions upon which no consensus has been reached. The New Right has fashioned a scenario of this demise that places the issue of education at the center of domestic problems and has rearticulated the issues in order to connect education to the broader political and economic objectives of a new conservativism. This scenario depends primarily on the strategy of disconnecting education from both its history as a platform for developing critical democratic citizenship and from any connection to primary state economic support for achieving educational equality and diversity.

George Bush announced his plan for educational policy in the fall of 1991, a significantly late entry into the issue considering that he declared himself the "education president" in his 1988 campaign. This plan consists of three main proposals: (1) implement repetitive and constant nationwide testing and evaluation (especially in math and science); (2) channel public monies from support for public schools in order to enable parents to choose private schools; (3) establish pilot projects in which business interests develop new models for educational development. Despite some differences, the Clinton administration, thus far, is still operating from the same general premises of this plan.

This platform follows from a particular scenario of the demise of education that links together the concerns of the new conservative alliance (consisting of right-wing religious fundamentalists, neoconservatives and free-market conservatives). This scenario articulates the demise of American education as a loss of technical skills that has led to the slide in economic productivity in comparison to other industrial nations such as Japan and Germany, and as a loss of a consensus on American cultural values, that is, individualism, hard work, the family, and so on. These losses are attributed to the failure of the liberal programs of education implemented in the 1960s, as well as the more general liberal practice of solving problems by "throwing money at them." This scenario sees liberal education programs (actually rooted much earlier in the foundations of American public education and advanced in the work of Dewey and others) as undercutting cultural values and work skills through its emphasis on student experience, individualized learning, multicultural education, and so forth. Further, the liberal calls for a rethinking of tiers, standardized testing and other classroom structures has led to a lack of discipline and a questioning of authority that undercuts the conservative agenda.

We can see how Bush's "solutions" square with this interpretation: the call for testing reimposes discipline and surveillance within the classroom (this strategy is bolstered by Bush's emphasis on parental control as crucial to his program) and eradicates multiculturalism by imposing a common curriculum; the call for redistributing funds from the public sector to the private sector reinstitutes the educational goals of the wealthy and powerful in maintaining a division between educating an elite leadership, while training the masses for menial tasks; the call for links between education and industry furthers these goals and excuses the administration's lack of funding for education by shifting the focus to management efficiency and private funding for productivity-enhancing styles of learning.

These outward strategies of the Bush administration are rearticulated and bolstered by the further work of conservative factions in setting the agenda for cultural politics. The right-wing religious fundamentalists and moral traditionalists have directed their attacks against liberalism's godlessness and the supposed loss of a natural cultural consensus rooted in Judeo-Christian values. For education this means a return to "family values," school prayer, discipline and the transcendental truths of American commitment to freedom and equality. The neoconservatives emphasize the need for America to regain its lost "golden age" of economic and moral superiority. This leads to a twofold purpose for education: the training of technical experts in the sciences and math in order to restore us to a position of superior economic productivity, and a return to the "traditional" values of the nation in order to support and insure the continuance of the economic project. The free-market conservatives emphasize that privatization equals profit—economic and cultural. For education, this means that state intervention is the enemy.

As Lawrence Grossberg (1992) notes, all of these factions have coalesced with the current administration and with industry to form an alliance that supports a particular direction in political and ideological struggles:

To redefine "freedom" and reconstitute the boundaries of civil liberties, to (re)regulate sexual and gender roles (leading to the construction of ever more violent antifeminist and homophobic positions); to monitor and even isolate particular segments of the population, especially various racial and ethnic minorities who, along with women and children, make up the vast majority of the poor; and to discipline the working class (e.g., through attacks on unions) in order to (de)regulate an international consumer economy dedicated to the increasing accumulation of profit (without the apparent necessity of converting wealth into investment). (10)

The New Right aims to reverse the various progressive policies put in place in the last twenty years by fashioning an affective alliance that combines the disparate interests of economic elites, moral authoritarians and cold war conservatives. As Henry Giroux (1988, 5) puts it, "Under the rubric of acknowledging the problems that characterize everyday existence, they have further undermined the possibility of democratic life by perpetuating what Bloch has called the 'swindle of fulfillment.' " These strategies of the New Right have important implications for the future of higher education (and particularly, for our purposes, the direction of the university and media education's place in it).

For university education, the primary issues are the definition of the goals and purposes of higher education, the extent to which multicultural issues and curricula are addressed and implemented, and the definition of the work of the intellectual/teacher in the university. The New Right's general strategy is to disconnect higher education from any concern with developing civic learning and public responsibility for the purpose of engendering new possibilities for democratic participation. Instead, university education is conceived as a platform for instilling moral regulation through enshrining the virtues of "possessive individualism, the struggle for advantage, and the legitimation of forms of knowledge that restrict the possibility for political understanding and action" (Giroux, 1988, 21). Second, the New Right defines the purposes of university education in terms of economic productivity through technical and skills training to be accomplished through the further implementation of business and military research. Ironically, Bush's push for education calls for no increase in federal funding for higher education. In conjunction with general economic hard times and decreased enrollments, this has resulted in state university systems being hit with catastrophic funding shortfalls that have led to hiring freezes, reduction in courses, departments and faculty positions, and so on. This pushes the state universities into a position where they will either have to increase their ties to business or perish. It is yet to be seen if the Clinton administration will reverse this trend in funding, but the economic plan to cut the deficit will certainly cut short a sweeping increase in funding.

Further, the New Right has mobilized a nationwide campaign against multicultural education and any pedagogical practice that addresses the relationships between equality, diversity and democratic citizenship. This campaign has been conducted under the rubric of "political correctness," an empty signifier used to attack any position that does not advance the moral and political goals of the new conservativism. The New Right has constructed a complex network of think tanks, conservative educational organizations, media publications and links to national media that has effectively defined multiculturism and political discourse as itself the problem. This mobilized effort has put the Left on the defensive and has shifted the discourse of education away from the progressive agenda that connected higher education to the engendering of an egalitarian and diverse public sphere in the service of radical democracy. As Giroux puts it,

The argument often expressed by mainstream educators that any form of oppositional discourse by default represents an imposition of one's views on somebody else is similar to the nineteenth-century ruling-class view that one could not raise one's voice, struggle politically, or promote social criticism because it violated the "gentlemanly" codes of civility. . . . Not only does such a discourse ignore the political nature of all schooling and pedagogy, it also represents an apology for forms of pedagogy that in their claims to neutrality merely voice the interests of the status quo and the logic of the dominant ideologies. (1988, 70)

The New Right's educational discourse on "political correctness" calls for an unreflective celebration of American cultural sameness, a view of authority rooted in the status of natural truths and in the status of the teacher as transmitter of those truths, and in a curriculum that fosters the interests of market imperatives.

Finally, the strategy of the New Right discourse on education calls for a particular definition of the place of the intellectual/teacher. Again, any critical function of the university is attacked as partisan. Instead, practicing academics must above all be objective and neutral. This reduces the role of the intellectual to reciting given cultural values and training future "producers" in the job skills they will need to take up their place in the "new world order." Concretely, we have seen New Right cultural critics, administration spokesmen and even state legislatures calling for a reduction in the research role for academics and for increased teaching roles. Academics, in sum, should not be intellectuals at all, but rather conduits for training employable consumers. Of course, primary research in the sciences and engineering remain untouched by this, for any practice with direct "productive" results can be connected to the primary economic motives of the new conservative program.

These are the current plans for higher education within the dominant position of the New Right and their significance for the future of university education is obvious. This programmatic discourse also sets the context for the development of media education and its place within the university. The future of media education, media studies, communication education, and so on will be, in part, determined by how those designing and carrying out curricula in these fields deal with these issues. The history of media education to this point has tended to develop along lines that point it in a direction that fully squares with these New Right directives. We will deal more explicitly with this issue in the chapters that follow, but at this point we can see how media education is situated in this discourse by its emphasis on professionalism, its generally acritical stance toward the media in assuming its status as a fourth estate, its self-definition as both a science and technical program, its ties to the media industry through internships and industry-related accreditation programs, and its separation of practical course work from theoretical course work.

In describing the New Right's scenario for educational practice we have defined the context that any alternative or oppositional educational philosophy must consider and, in effect, define itself against. It is this pedagogy that alternative voices in educational philosophy are directed against. Particularly, what has become known as "critical pedagogical theory" begins by examining and critically evaluating the traditional definitions of what education should be. It is this body of thought, as laid out by Paulo Freire, Henry Giroux, Peter McLaren, Michael Apple, Michelle Fine, Valerie Walkerdine, and others, that we will examine as offering possibilities for redefining education as an emancipatory practice against the grain of the antidemocratic, technicist, managerial proposals of the New Right. It is this work, particularly, that opens up the possibilities for media education to be conceived as aiding in the construction of a multicultural, egalitarian, critical and radical democratic society.

THE FOUNDATIONS OF CRITICAL PEDAGOGICAL THEORY

> The major objective of critical pedagogy is to empower students to intervene in their own self-formation and to transform the oppressive features of the wider society that make such an intervention necessary. (McLaren, 1988, xi)

The present state of media education is the result of a number of factors—historical, political and cultural—that have placed it in a precarious position within the contemporary university: (1) its relative newness and thus, lower status in comparison to classical fields such as English literature, chemistry, and so on; (2) its interdisciplinary nature and the efforts nevertheless to form it into a discipline with an object, method and curricular structure modeled on the social science disciplines; (3) its other history as a practical field with industry connections and professional training goals; (4) its contemporary ferment in confronting and using critical methods borrowed from other fields (cultural studies, structuralism, literary criticism, etc.); (5) its obvious connections to the so-called information revolution and the efforts arising from this to define it as a technical discipline; and (6) the meeting of all of these histories with the present educational plans of the New Right through the adoption of traditional pedagogical models.

It is our contention that media education needs to rethink its position and that critical pedagogy offers the tools for such a rethinking. In the remainder of this chapter we will lay out the general principles of critical pedagogy and attempt to deal with those aspects of its theoretical work—rooted in a language of critique and of possibility—that are most pertinent to media education. This treatment of critical pedagogy will serve two purposes: to introduce the field to those within media education who have little knowledge of this work and to lay the groundwork for our substantive critique of the present state of media education.

Critical Pedagogy's Task: Critique and Democracy

Cultural Politics

Peter McLaren (1989, 158) foregrounds a crucial choice that we must make in regard to our conceptions of education: "Do we want our schools to create a passive, risk-free citizenry, or a politicized citizenry, capable of fighting for various forms of public life and informed by a concern for equality and social justice? Despite the obvious rhetorical nature of this question, it still must be pointed out that conservative *and* liberal views of education have paid only lip service to the democratization of schooling. On the other hand, critical pedagogy, as it has developed over the last twenty years, has foregrounded the political and moral choice for a radically democratic form of education. McLaren summarizes the practice of critical pedagogical theory as follows:

Critical pedagogy examines schools both in their historical context and as part of the existing social and political fabric that characterizes the dominant society. Critical pedagogy poses a variety of important counterlogics to the positivistic, ahistorical, and depoliticized analysis employed by both liberal and conservative critics of schooling—an analysis all too readily visible in the training programs in our colleges of education. Fundamentally concerned with the centrality of politics and power in our understanding of how schools work, critical theorists have produced work centering on the political economy of schooling, the state of education, the representation of texts, and the construction of student subjectivity. (1989, 159)

In carrying out this work, critical pedagogy draws upon the work of the Frankfurt School of critical theory, the work of Paulo Freire in extending critical theory to the practice of development education, and more recently, the contemporary theoretical contributions of feminism, cultural studies, poststructuralism, postcolonialism and postmodernism. These diverse roots of critical pedagogy point to the fact that it is not a homogeneous body of thought, nor a clearly defined discipline, but rather an open field of study united in its concern for critically challenging the dominant practice and theory of education.

Critical pedagogy begins by describing schooling as a form of *cultural politics*, that is, that education is a political phenomenon and that pedagogy is present in all spheres of society. It must be clearly seen that pedagogy is not simply about curriculum design, teaching techniques and evaluation methods; it is also and fundamentally about how knowledge is constructed in relations of power—how things got to be the way they are and how they might be transformed. Neither is education simply about increasing cognitive capacities, honing work skills, developing literacy or memorizing a body of neutral knowledge for personal development. In this light, a critical pedagogy for media education must start from the realization that any system of education is a political way of maintaining or modifying the appropriation of discourses, along with the power and knowledge they carry.

Traditional and liberal theories of education describe schooling as a neutral process of the acquisition of language and related skills that provide the means for equal opportunity. But as Michel Foucault states,

Education may well be, as of right, the instrument whereby every individual, in a society like our own, can gain access to any kind of discourse. But we all know that in its distribution, in what it permits and prevents, it follows the well-trodden battle lines of social conflict. Every educational system is a political means of maintaining or modifying the appropriation of discourse with the knowledge and powers it carries with it. (1972, 227)

The work of Samuel Bowles and Herbert Gintis (1976) and Michael Apple (1990) has painstakingly documented and criticized the political economic dimension of schooling—the manner in which it has served the interests of capital in a class-based meritocracy that reproduces inequality, racism and sexism; and the way it fragments labor through the teaching of competitiveness, acquiescence to authority and cultural ethnocentrism. Henry Giroux (Giroux & McLaren, 1989, 127) extends this analysis to the whole cultural field, which includes: the institutional practices in which schools (and other pedagogical sites) reproduce the logic of capital through forms of privilege and domination; the representational practices that produce and reproduce particular ways of life; and the forms of consciousness, experience and desire through which agents produce, appropriate and struggle over the forms of meaning produced through pedagogical practices.

These aspects of educational critique apply directly to media education. We need to ask tough questions about where our economic allegiances are, how we contribute to the production of a cheap labor force for broadcast industries, and how we reproduce a "media professional" consciousness through our practical curricula. These issues will be discussed in chapters 3, 4 and 5.

In its cultural politics, critical pedagogy does not remain at the moment of critique. In fact, its whole project is defined through an emancipatory interest rooted in a radical theory of ethics aimed at transforming the nature of schooling. This project is historically rooted in the democratic school of education, represented by John Dewey, particularly in his conception of education as serving the renewal of democracy, and the revitalization of public life. This project is extended in Paulo Freire's pedagogy of liberation and its fundamental commitment to dialogue and community as the basis for a transformative educational praxis. In Freire's literacy projects he foregrounds the oppressive conditions that constrain impoverished groups and engenders a dialogue that enables them to read the world in order to reshape it.

Thus, for theorists working within the traditions of critical pedagogy, a given curriculum represents a site of struggle, structured around silenced and omitted voices; it represents struggles over competing versions of the past, present and future. Critical pedagogy represents a partisan project linking the purpose of schooling to a transformative vision of the future, a project, however, no more partisan than that representative of neoconservative interests in the preservation and enhancement of existing power relations. Critical pedagogy need not apologize for its partisan position, for as we have attempted to show, all pedagogical practices are rooted in politics. Traditional conceptions of education that see it as a neutral provider of skills are theoretically and empirically indefensible. To live in this value-neutral world is to be divorced from reality. The theories, policies and practices of education are inherently "ethical and political and they ultimately involve intensely personal choices about 'the common good' " (Apple, 1990, viii).

Redefining Pedagogy

It must be made clear that in critical pedagogy's project, pedagogy is not simply about "teaching technique," but refers to all those practices that define what is important to know, how it is to be known and how this production of knowledge constructs social identities. The pedagogical is about "how relations of pedagogy and relations of power are inextricably tied not only to what people know but how they come to know it in a particular way within the constraints of specific social forms" (Giroux & Simon, 1989, 2). In this perspective we cannot talk about teaching without talking about politics. Thus, critical pedagogy must link itself to the goals of a radical democracy, it must engage and critique the conditions of knowledge production and it must provide a language of possibility for transforming those conditions.

The politicized notion of pedagogy extends the sphere of pedagogical practice beyond the school: "any practice which intentionally tries to influence the production of meaning is a pedagogical practice" (Giroux & Simon, 1989, 230). Thus, the pedagogical is practiced not just in the schools, but in the family, public discourse, the church, the media, and so on. A critical pedagogy must address these spheres in its explication of education, as well as "what happens in schools." For our analysis of media education this becomes a crucial point.

In the context of higher education, a thorough explication of the concept of pedagogy begins with an analysis of its undertheorization. Outside of its own literature, pedagogy has been underdefined as little more than a referent to teaching "style," cast in terms of personality and temperament, mechanics and classroom control. Critical pedagogy, in its metaquestioning of instructional practice, leads one to view the classroom not only as a site of instruction, but as a cultural arena, that is, as a site of cultural struggle in which various sociological and ideological struggles are continually being played out. As Giroux states,

Such an emphasis does not at all diminish pedagogy's concern with "What's to be done?" As a complex and extensive term, *pedagogy's* concern includes the integration in practice of particular curriculum content and design, classroom strategies and techniques, a time and space for the practice of those strategies and techniques, and evaluation purposes and methods. . . . But the discourse of pedagogy centers something more. It stresses that the realities of what happens in classrooms organize a view of how a teacher's work within an institutional context specifies a particular version of what knowledge is of most worth, in what direction we should desire, what it means to know something, and how we might construct representations of ourselves, others, and our physical and social environment. (Giroux & McLaren, 1989, 239)

This conception of pedagogy asks that the various assumptions underlying, for example, the production values of dominant news and entertainment media, be critically assessed as an integral part of the instructional process of a "hands-on" course on television. This is not simply a matter of including attention to "critical thinking" within the existing curriculum. As McLaren (1989) has noted, in their use of the concept of "critical thinking," both neoconservatives and liberals have removed from the term "critical" its political and cultural dimensions (resulting in an undertheorized meaning as "thinking skills"). In these terms, pedagogy is again reduced to the process by which students are provided with a set of cognitive skills. In the case of media production, these skills include equipment operation and general indoctrination into the techniques of classical/dominant entertainment production.

In its pronounced tendency toward metaquestioning, critical pedagogy expresses a concern for the antecedent *moral* dimensions involved in the use to which these skills are eventually put. McLaren has argued that the tradition of critical pedagogy is "founded on the conviction that schooling for self and social empowerment is ethically prior to a mastery of technical skills" (1989, 162). As the dominant power relations of race, class, gender and sexual preference are reproduced, moment by moment, in popular film and television, university educators whose value-neutral and atheoretical pedagogy has trained a generation of media (re)production students and (value) maintenance engineers must be asked to examine the wider and unavoidable political dimensions of their efforts. As teachers of mass communication this suggests the potential impact of the project of critical pedagogy upon our professional, personal and political lives.

This questioning of the social functions of knowledge leads us to ask a number of further questions about the nature of our pedagogy: What is the connection between social class and knowledge taught in school? Why do we value scientific knowledge over other forms? What accounts for some knowledge having high status and "practical value," while other forms of knowledge are marginalized and discredited? How have certain pedagogical practices become so ingrained that we accept them as natural? And, as McLaren states: "To what extent do such pedagogical practices work as forms of social control that support, stabilize, and legitimate the role of the teacher as a moral gatekeeper of the state? What are the functions and effects of the systematic imposition of ideological perspectives on classroom teaching practices?" (1989, 179). This questioning against the grain is an important part of a pedagogical project for media education, and we will address each of these questions in our analysis.

Radical Democracy and the Public Sphere

The notion that higher education should advance the goals of democracy is a given, but neoconservative and liberal theories of education have gone nowhere in defining what democracy is. Neither have these viewpoints explained what the role of education is in the development of democracy. Neoconservatives are content to leave democracy underdefined and to assume that it already exists. Education for democracy, then, is simply a matter of reproducing the present state of affairs and rehearsing the givens of current political rhetoric. For liberals, democracy does involve the development of participation in political affairs, and education takes its place in this through the personal development of the student. However, John Dewey's notion of creative democracy and education as supportive of social construction and the revitalization of community has disappeared from current liberal viewpoints. In the current liberal rhetoric, democracy functions in the political institutions of U.S. society, but the inegalitarian, hierarchical constitution of the economy is ignored. Education serves the purpose of equalizing economic chances. As Bowles and Gintis (1976, 26) put it,

Poverty and inequality, in this view, are the consequences of individual choice or personal inadequacies, not the normal outgrowths of our economic institutions. The problem, clearly, is to fix up the people, not to change the economic structures which regulate their lives. Despite persistent setbacks in practice, the liberal faith in the equalizing power of schooling has dominated both intellectual and policy circles. Education has been seen . . . as the "great equalizer."

For critical pedagogy, any theory of education must be situated in the greater context of economic, political and cultural practices. This requires rethinking education's relationship to the economic and the extent to which the development of political democracy requires also the reconstitution of economic structures in a democratic form. But what do we mean by "democracy" in the first place?

The conception of democracy must be pushed beyond the current under-theorization in which the goals of democracy are defined in terms of individual rights to opportunity as set by the free market, equality before the law, and the right to representative government through a truncated participation, defined as the right to vote. In forming a more radical definition of democracy, we can begin with McLaren's description that, "Generally speaking, democracy is defined at the level of social formations, political communities, and social practices which are regulated by principles of social justice, equality, and diversity" (1988, xvii).

A radical democracy, then, begins with a radical critique of current forms of representation that limit the populace's decision making to choices over who will govern. Instead, we must begin with the principle that individuals and communities should have a direct role in the determination of the conditions of their own lives: "they should enjoy equal rights in the specification of the framework which generates and limits the opportunities available to them" (Held, 1987, 290). Thus, a radical democracy extends participation to the spheres of the cultural, the economic and the social.

Within a radical democracy the place of education is redefined and reinvigorated. First of all, we must take up Paulo Freire's distinction between schooling and education. Schooling is primarily a form of social control in which the forms of pedagogy normalize subjects to take up places as skilled citizens in the given social order. Education, on the other hand, serves as a form of potential transformation in which the forms of pedagogy allow for active subjects committed to self- and social empowerment (Freire, 1989). Thus, a critical pedagogy calls for a democratic curriculum. Such a curriculum would not be defined in terms of the abstract categories of various isolated disciplines (history, English literature, etc.), but rather would incorporate themes and issues that address the concrete conditions and problems of adult life.

Such knowledge should include not only the basic skills students will need to work and live in the wider society, but also knowledge about the social forms through which human beings live, become conscious, and sustain themselves, particularly with respect to the social and political demands of democratic citizenship. This relates to knowledge about power and how it works, as well as to analyses of those practices such as racism, sexism, and class exploitation that structure and mediate the encounters of everyday life. (Giroux, 1988, 103)

In this redefinition of the place of education in democratic development, schools are seen as *democratic public spheres*, that is, as institutions whose work is not to reproduce a labor force for a preestablished industry, nor to ensure the transmission of a consensual cultural formation, but rather to "perform public service essential to the democratic state" (McLaren, 1989, 238). Thus, the practice of pedagogy must be seen as extending beyond the walls of the classroom and the university. Critical educators' development of vital strategies that effectively confront the space of political authority established by the Right must be based in a pedagogy that is grounded in a politics and view of authority that "argues for forms of community life which extend the principles of liberty, equality, justice, and freedom to the widest possible set of institutional and lived relations" (Giroux, 1991, 56). This means that those devoted to the redemocratization of society must rechannel their energies into developing new sites and new practices within public life. Giroux stresses the importance of reestablishing the importance of the public sphere:

Academics can no longer retreat into their careers, classrooms, or symposiums as if they were the only public spheres available for engaging the power of ideas and the relations of power. Foucault's (1977) notion of the specific intellectual taking up struggles connected to particular issues and contexts must be combined with Gramsci's (1971) notion of the engaged intellectual who connects his or her work to broader social concerns that deeply affect how people live, work and survive. (Giroux, 1991, 57)

This widening of arenas is crucial, both in the sense that various groups (multicultural, feminist, political, etc.) have a chance to convince others that their concerns should be added to the agenda of the common good and in the sense of expanding the discursive space of practice to include both public opinion-formation and decision making. Important, here, is Nancy Fraser's (1990) notion of *weak publics* and *strong publics*. Weak publics function outside of decision-making institutions (in the intellectual arena in such decentralized, collectively organized projects as journals, bookstores, conferences, professional organizations, etc.) and function primarily at the level of opinion-formation. Strong publics, on the other hand, encompass both opinion-formation and decision making and are carried out within existing state institutions, including bureaucracies (National Endowment for the Humanities, Federal Communications Commission, etc.) and universities.[1]

Rita Felski (1989, 167) has described how discourses work in the public sphere in the case of feminism. In some ways, the diversity of feminist practice stands as an example of widening the arena of public action. It has functioned in diverse institutional locations, from grassroots opinion-forming collectives, to state institutions, to women's refuges and advisory centers that function semiautonomously within the framework of bureaucracies (Felski, 1989, 170). As Felski reiterates,

Given the complex interpenetrations of state and society in late capitalism, one can no longer postulate the ideal of a public sphere which can function outside existing commercial and state institutions and at the same time claim an influential and representative function as a forum for oppositional activity and debate. Instead, the category of the feminist public sphere needs to be effective across a range of levels both outside and inside existing institutional structures, for example, by exploiting the contradictory critical spaces within the education system. (1989, 171)

For critical educators and intellectuals this means working for and with "the masses" to rediscover those issues and struggles that really matter. In the end, an effective Left politics must be affective, it must work toward reinvigorating public debate through a passionate discourse. In Giroux's words,

The struggle against racism, class structures, and sexism needs to move away from simply a language of critique and redefine itself as part of a language of transformation and hope. This suggests that educators combine with others engaged in public struggles in order to invent languages and provide spaces both in and out of schools that offer new opportunities for social movements to come together in order to rethink and re-experience democracy as a struggle over values, practices, social relations, and subject positions which enlarge the terrain of human capacities and possibilities as a basis for a compassionate social order. At issue here is the need to create a politics which contributes to the multiplication of sites of democratic struggles, sites which affirm specific struggles while recognizing the necessity to embrace broader issues that enhance the life of the planet while extending the spirit of democracy to all societies. (1991, 57)

Media educators in mass communication departments need to ask why we have forged connections with broadcast industries, advertising agencies, mainstream news outlets and university sports complexes, rather than with public access centers, community action groups, broad-based arts coalitions and forms of alternative media. We need to think about which private/public spheres we really want to be an influence on and how these spheres fit with our pedagogical practice.

Key Concepts for Rethinking Higher Education

Our conception of media education will be rooted in the overall task of critical pedagogy that we have just articulated. This rethinking of media education will begin with a first step of criticizing the present practice of media education. This practice is rooted in a number of material and theoretical practices that have defined the direction of higher education in general. A number of critical pedagogy's theoretical concepts have a direct bearing on this critique of the historical constitution of the university and the present practices that have resulted from this foundation. These concepts apply to a variety of issues that function across a wide spectrum of practices, from the concrete practice of teaching and the formation of curriculum, to the definition of liberal education, the function of the university and the place of intellectuals in its formation and practice.

We will now lay out some of these concepts in their general application. We will then proceed to a brief description of critical pedagogy's application to the specifics of media education.

The Banking Concept, the Hidden Curriculum and Critical Literacy

The neoconservative philosophy of education calls for a "back to basics" approach, which, in effect, entails both a reestablishment of the traditional authority of the teacher and the parallel authority of an "objective" curriculum. This view has called for the removal of politics from schooling and the return to a supposedly naturally arrived at canon of texts that contain verifiably "true" knowledge. Ultimately, such a program is rooted in a *transmission* model of education. This model is representative of a set of instrumentalized relations in which the learner is positioned as a passive blank slate, the teacher as value-neutral transmitter, and knowledge as a body of immutable information waiting to be passed along. Paulo Freire (1989) has referred to this model as the banking concept of pedagogy, a model in which education becomes

an act of depositing, in which the students are the depositories and the teacher is the depositor. Instead of communicating, the teacher issues communiques and makes deposits which the students patiently receive, memorize, and repeat. . . . In the banking concept of education, knowledge is a gift bestowed by those who consider themselves knowledgeable upon those whom they consider to know nothing. (1989, 58)

It is clear that the neoconservative call for fixed canons, discipline, value-neutral methods and standardized evaluation are rooted in the banking model and result in the regulation and control of the way the world "enters into" the students (Freire, 1989, 62). This view is further rooted in a traditional conception of culture as a given body of information with a fixed meaning, which everyone recognizes as the common culture, necessary for building the life of the nation. Such a view, expressed in the works of E. D. Hirsch (1987), Allan Bloom (1987), and others, ignores the relationship of culture to power and political practices. As Stanley Aronowitz and Henry Giroux point out,

A more critical understanding of the relationship between culture and schooling would start with a definition of culture as a set of activities by which different groups produce collective memories, knowledge, social relations, and values within historically constituted relations of power. Culture is about the production and legitimation of particular ways of life, and schools often transmit a culture that is specific to class, gender, and race. (1991, 50)

The neoconservatives want to erase any foregrounding of their own politics and power positions and to focus on curriculum as simply choices over programs of study, course syllabi and texts. Critical pedagogy conceives of curriculum as much more than this; it is the introduction to forms of life that play a crucial part in defining who will benefit from the economic and political arrangements in society. Critical educators have referred to this as the *hidden curriculum*. The hidden curriculum refers to the order of effects of schooling that lie outside of the stated goals of transmitting knowledge for skills and literacy. As McLaren defines it,

The hidden curriculum also includes teaching and learning styles that are emphasized in the classroom, the messages that get transmitted to the student by the total physical and instructional environment, governance structures, teacher expectations, and grading procedures. The hidden curriculum deals with the tacit ways in which knowledge and behavior get constructed, outside the usual course materials and formally scheduled lessons. It is a part of the bureaucratic and managerial "press" of the school—the combined forces by which students are induced to comply with dominant ideologies and social practices related to authority, behavior, and morality. (1989, 183–84)

In opposition to the depoliticization of education called for by the neoconservative imposition of the banking model and the concomitant erasure of the hidden curriculum, critical pedagogy calls for a project of *critical literacy*. The work of Paulo Freire, for instance, calls for a practice of *conscientization*, a participatory model of learning based on a genuine dialogue between teachers and students, who work from the basis of their own experiences to struggle with competing interpretations of the world. This problem-posing approach has been extended in critical pedagogy to a more comprehensive project of critical literacy. This project moves beyond traditional notions of literacy as the acquisition of language skills and the neoconservative extension of this platform into technical skill training, the imposition of disciplined English language usage, and indoctrination into cultural literacy defined as the ability to recite a canon of prescribed texts. Critical literacy, on the other hand,

involves decoding the ideological dimensions of texts, institutions, social practices, and cultural forms such as television and film, in order to reveal their selective interests. The purpose behind acquiring this type of literacy is to create a citizenry critical enough to both analyze and challenge the oppressive characteristics of the larger society so that a more just, equitable, and democratic society can be created. (McLaren, 1989, 196)

Empowerment and Student Voice

The replacement of the banking concept of education with critical literacy calls for a further reconception of the position of the student. A truly liberatory pedagogy must be rooted in the purpose of empowering students to become literate about their own histories and experiences and to appropriate and rework the codes and cultures of dominant spheres in a manner that enables them to transcend their own environments (Freire and Macedo, 1987, 47). This calls for a transformation of the relationship of teacher authority and student receptivity from one where the student is conceived as an empty vessel to one where the student's voice is respected and developed.

Education as empowerment means more than giving students the tools to take up a place in an already constructed system of labor; it means providing the means by which students can rethink their relationships to the world of work and develop abilities as critical citizens, working toward a more just and equitable democracy. In traditional education the student is given the tools, techniques and formats for expression. Here, the student is a silent body that is given an imposed position from which to speak. Only after being inculcated with the dominant grammars of producing discourse can the student say anything. By imposing a predetermined state of rules and discursive categories the teacher gives the student the proper position from which to speak. The assumption is that the student has no valid voice until he or she learns the valorized modes of producing discourse (there is no better example of this practice than the prototypical media production course).

A critical pedagogy, instead, seeks to understand how subject positions are constructed for students through historically produced social forms that embody particular interests (Giroux, 1988, xxxv). This provides students with the opportunity to evaluate critically the limitations that have been placed on their own attempts to articulate their everyday experiences. In a critical pedagogy the task is to design curricula that give students an active and critical voice.

Students must be able to speak with their own voices, before they learn how to move outside of their own frames of reference, before they can break from the common sense that prevents them from understanding the socially constructed sources underlying their own self-formative processes and what it means to both challenge the latter and break with them. (Giroux, 1988, 203)

Pedagogy must begin, then, not with a canon of given knowledge or list of skills to be learned, but rather with the problems and needs of the students themselves. This does not mean that student experiences should be unqualifiedly valorized, but rather that the different voices that students employ to give meaning to their experiences should be respected and examined. Neither does this mean totally eradicating the authority of the teacher's voice. Instead,

The emancipatory power of a teacher's authoritative voice is exercised when a student's voice is allowed to assert itself so as to be both confirmed and analyzed, in terms of the particular values and ideologies that it represents. In the latter instance, the teacher voice can provide a critical context within which students can understand the various social forces and configurations of power that have helped give shape to their voices. . . . Such a pedagogy begins with the assumption that the stories that schools, teachers, and students construct can form the basis for a variety of approaches to teaching and learning in which hope and power play integral roles. (McLaren, 1989, 231)

The neoconservative model of pedagogy would, instead, sustain and even further the unquestioned voice of authority and the silencing of student voice. This is instituted in the practices of constructing taboo voices, closing down and smoothing over conversations, creating dichotomies between personal and social voice, and appropriating dissent (Fine, 1989). The silencing of student voice is further evident in the creation of false dichotomies such as theory versus practice, high versus low culture, objective versus subjective knowledge, and school pedagogy versus cultural pedagogy. This is most evident in the New Right's animosity toward popular culture (see Bloom, 1987), in which forms of popular culture (which are directly a part of student experience and commitment) are denigrated as deformed cultural practices or even as contributors to deviancy. Critical pedagogy, on the other hand, must engage with the popular as the background that informs students' engagement with any pedagogical encounter. This is not simply a matter of criticizing popular culture in order to devalorize student experiences, but rather, taking it up in the classroom in a manner in which it both gives validity to student experiences and interrogates those experiences in relation to cultural politics.

Transformative Intellectuals

More and more the university seems unable to fulfill its role in supporting and nourishing culture; nor has it fulfilled its role in providing skills for its "clients" to acquire jobs. The ideal of the university as a haven for the disinterested contemplation of culture in which its students and faculty take up the responsibility for advancing humane and civilized thought no longer seems possible or desirable (if it ever was). University education has become a given for the middle and upper classes and in its growth has diminished in idealistic appeal. Further, the idea that university education is a proven pathway to employment holds less and less validity. This notion of producing jobs for graduates has been instrumental in the rise of mass communication education, for example, but the actual vocational skills learned in these programs are more and more out of date, and the employment outlook in the field has diminished. The promise of a job is simply a false promise.

Within this crisis of the university the position of the intellectual, the faculty member, is in danger of losing its credibility and its raison d'etre. For growing numbers of the general public, intellectuals in the university either produce esoteric research incomprehensible and useless for the "real world," or they are promulgating an ideology of liberalism that threatens to undermine the fabric of society. More and more the function of public intellectual is given over to those working in think tanks (predominantly right wing) and the role of university intellectuals is being reconceived as that of technicians, whose primary function is implementing pedagogical practice. In this neoconservative scenario, university faculty should return to their role as intellectuals, in the sense that they carry forward the mission of the nation, and of course to their role as teachers, who reproduce the workforce.

For critical pedagogy, if the university is to overcome this "crisis" (which is as much a crisis of representation as a reality), it must revitalize the function of the professoriate as both public intellectuals and critical teachers. The accomplishment of this goal depends on reconceptualizing the school as a public sphere essential in developing a critical democracy in which teachers take up a role as transformative intellectuals whose scholarly work and pedagogical practice serve to educate students to become active citizens. Further, the work of teachers should be extended outside the university to other institutional and community spheres. As transformative intellectuals, teachers become public intellectuals, working to extend the concern for social justice and equality through a repoliticization of pedagogy and a pedagogical politics.

In and outside of the university, the practice of transformative intellectuals needs to be connected to political and cultural struggle, but this is not a call for intellectuals to be prophets that compel all people to step in line. The intellectual, instead, describes how things have gone thus far, but in such a way that possible paths of alliance are delineated (Foucault, 1989, 191). The intellectual participates in the formation of a political will by reproblematizing familiar discourses and practices in the direction of a "transformation constantly agitated by a permanent criticism" (Foucault, 1988, 155). The intellectual takes up a pedagogical function in the transformation of thought. His or her role "is to see how far the liberation of thought can make those transformations urgent enough for people to want to carry them out and difficult enough to carry out for them to be profoundly rooted in reality" (Foucault, 1988, 155). The authority of the intellectual Left must thus mobilize, by connecting its transformation of the "politics of truth" to an affective force.

Revitalizing the role of the intellectual will require a critique and reconceptualizing of the role of the university as neither a producer of "good" citizens, who take up their roles in the neoconservative scheme of politics and technological growth, nor as simply a bastion of liberal arts. We will address these issues in our analysis in chapter 4.

CRITICAL PEDAGOGY AND MEDIA EDUCATION

All of the issues presented in our description of critical pedagogy need to be addressed in critically analyzing media education: its place in the university and within the liberal arts, its relationship to economic influence, its position in cultural politics, its hidden curriculum, its self-definition as a particular form of pedagogy, its maintenance of a professional model of curriculum (and the influence of transmission models of pedagogy), its definitions of the media's and its own democratic practice, its practice in relation to student voice and multiculturalism, and its positioning of intellectuals who practice within it. We will address these and other issues in the chapters that follow.

Beyond these particular issues, critical pedagogy (particularly in its taking up of the concerns of cultural studies, poststructuralism and postmodernism) provides a potentially fruitful direction for media education in addressing the place of popular culture (including television, film and popular music) in the university.

A Critical Postmodernism

Any adequate account of the present practices of the media (and media education) must take into account the present historical conjuncture and thus must address the question of postmodernism. Critical pedagogy attempts to address the issues of the cultural politics of the media and their relationship to education through incorporating postmodern themes into an analysis that retains the political commitment of cultural studies as practiced by the Birmingham School (see chapter 2).

Postmodernism, as a form of cultural criticism and as a historical condition, directly challenges the project of modernism. We believe it rightly questions modernism's reliance on the notion of the autonomous individual, the emphasis on the linearity of thought, the aesthetic of rationality and order, the rationality of science in the process of progress, the preeminence of western European thought, and history as the process of the progress of Western culture. However, we cannot accept the postmodernist stance without question, we cannot simply accept its critique of modernism as total and final, nor can we simply meld the various "posts" together into a sweeping theory.

Postmodern theory makes us aware of how our subjectivity and experiences are constructed, how the meaning we attempt to grasp slips away in our failure to affectively commit to it, how our institutions and discursive formations lead us to erase difference and stand against the "other," and how the production of information and symbols has weakened the link between images and reality. While such a breaking down of our present condition can lead us to question that condition and resist it, there is also the very real potential within postmodern theory for it to lead to fatal strategies, wherein resistance is replaced by refusal, and critique by play.

This regressive postmodernism is most evident in Jean Baudrillard's (1988) burned out space of hyper-conformity, and the further aestheticization of his position by Arthur Kroker and David Cook (1988), in which the masses celebrate their own extermination in the black hole of television. Lost in this regressive version of postmodernism is any sense of how people struggle with the images and codes that confront them. Likewise, the affirmation of difference is disconnected from any account of how cultural, political and economic constraints position various groups in asymmetrical power relations. In short, a postmodernism that endlessly plays with literary texts, or maps out a world of simulations in which there is no place from which to speak, erases any critical sense of history or politics (Giroux, 1988, 24). A critical media education cannot exist under this view of the postmodern, for within the Baudrillardian space of the electronic simulation of reality the only strategy left for the subject is self-parody.

The bleak nihilism of postmodernist deconstruction must be connected to critical pedagogy's project of reconstruction (from out of the ashes looking back at the end of the world). The pessimism and despair that characterizes the postmodernism of Jameson, Lyotard and Baudrillard must be understood as emanating from the context of their own individual subject positions. For those whose lives have benefited through the occupation of a position of privilege within these various "grand narratives," the collapse of these structures; the unmasking of the once absolute and eternal as now arbitrary and transient; the retransformation of the natural back into the cultural; the collapse of the mythic back into the arena of the human and the political; all of this will most certainly find their response in phrases like "crisis," "the end of meaning," "the end of history," and so on. However, from the subject positions of those who have been excluded by these narratives, whose own voices have been silenced and marginalized, such a collapse may be experienced as liberatory and empowering (McClary, 1989/90). In other words, the response to these "collapses" may range from despair to celebration depending upon your location within a given set of asymmetrical power relations. And this opens up the possibility of a critical postmodernism.

It is in this sense that Dick Hebdige (1988) has argued that theories of the "post" have "no intrinsic political belonging in themselves" (51). While for Baudrillard, postmodernity is characterized by the utter annihilation of difference and the end of history and politics, a critical postmodernism is "identified with diversity and difference, a politics of contestation and change" (51). We must seek to connect postmodernism's notions of culture, difference and subjectivity with the modernist concerns for the language of public life, thus reaffirming a public philosophy that broadens and deepens individual liberties and rights through rather than against a radical notion of democracy. By drawing upon this politicized notion of the postmodern, the practice of media education can be seen to offer vital strategies.

If media education is to be advanced within a critical pedagogy, it must be conceived as a political, social and cultural practice. Thus, a critical theory of media education must propose it as an arena of practices that still offers strategies that can be taken seriously as vital. It is crucial, then, to distinguish between those postmodern positions that lead either to an aestheticization of politics or to a cultural pessimism, from that of a critical postmodernism offered by Giroux (1988):

At its best, a critical postmodernism wants to redraw the map of modernism so as to effect a shift in power from the privileged and the powerful to those groups struggling to gain a measure of control over their lives in what is increasingly becoming a world marked by a logic of disintegration. (162)

As such, a critical postmodernism integrates the elements of the modernist political project with the resistant strategies of postmodernism. As theoretical projects, both modernism and postmodernism are flawed in certain respects, and both need to be examined for strengths and weaknesses. In particular, the elements of modernism that link memory, agency and reason to the construction of a democratic public sphere need to be retained in the construction of a theory of media education for the present conditions of the postmodern world (Giroux, 1988, 6–7).

Given the above discussion, how can a project of critical media education be developed? The location of these matters within the terrain of postmodern cultural theory may help further to flesh out the character of our media pedagogy in postmodern late-capitalist America. On the one hand, the increasing development of science and technology provides the possibility of freeing humans from dehumanizing and back-breaking labor. In turn, this freedom offers humanity new opportunities for the development of, and access to, a culture that promotes a more critical and discriminatory sensibility in all modes of communication and experience. On the other hand, the development of technology and science, constructed according to the laws of capitalist rationality, has ushered in forms of domination and control that appear to thwart rather than extend the possibilities of human emancipation.

Given the existing social formation, the modes of communication are operated predominantly in the interests of oppression. This is not a simple mechanical operation but is tied to the hegemonic conjuncture of market, military and political interests. Within this grouping of interests the media serve to construct consensus and dissent,[2] to reconfigure the relationship of meaning and affect in the construction of a narrative of nation, to surveil the population and in so doing create systems of normalization and subjectification. However, this operation of the media is not a seamless operation closing off all possibilities of alternative use. The media, then, constitute a leaky system that is struggled over in its production and reception.

A critical pedagogy of media education begins with such an assessment of contemporary culture and the function of media within it. Foregrounded, here, is the nature of media as themselves pedagogical machines, which function in the defining of what counts as legitimate knowledge. A critical pedagogy adequate to the task of analyzing education's relation to media must begin with a theory that accounts for the potential of the media to serve the purposes of domination. At the same time, however, it cannot reject the possibilities for struggle with domination that occur in the pedagogical encounter with media, that is, in its production, reception and use. Critical pedagogy, then, has increasingly turned its attention to how education should deal with popular culture within an overall project for critical democratic education. Drawing upon cultural studies, critical pedagogy has raised three areas of inquiry that have a direct bearing on the project of a critical media education. First, popular culture as a significant practice in shaping student practices and their relations to forms of pedagogy and learning. How can popular culture be taken up in the classroom in a manner that both gives validity to student experiences and interrogates those experiences in relation to cultural politics? Second, how can popular culture itself be engaged as pedagogical? The politicized notion of pedagogy extends the sphere of pedagogical practice beyond the school to the media themselves. Third, as educators who teach courses directly on various aspects of popular culture, how should we conceive of our own pedagogical practice in dealing with popular culture? These three areas of inquiry are all interconnected in their concerns and mutually inform each other.

Media, Popular Culture and the Encounter with Schooling

Our discussion is grounded in the assertion that educational theory must engage with the popular as the background that informs students' engagement with any pedagogical encounter. In this encounter, however, the distancing dichotomy of high versus low culture must be avoided. As we have already noted, this is not simply a matter of either criticizing popular culture for the purpose of devalorizing student experience, or obversely celebrating the popular in an acritical acceptance. Rather, as Henry Giroux and Roger Simon (1989) suggest, we must consider popular culture as the background of knowledge forms and affective instruments that ground student "voice" (243).

This involves seeing culture as a contested terrain—a field of struggle, in which the production, legitimation and circulation of particular forms of meaning and experience are central areas of conflict and battle (Giroux & McLaren, 1989, 126). Popular culture, then, is both a site of struggle between dominant and subordinant groups and a reference for understanding how experience is organized and produced in the dynamics of everyday life (Giroux & Simon, 1989, 244). Students' everyday lives are, in part, constituted by their affective investments in popular culture.

This suggests that educators make popular culture a legitimate object of school knowledge so as to deepen the relationship between schooling and everyday life and to better grasp as a basis for critical analysis the totality of elements that organize student identities, experiences, and cultures. (Giroux & McLaren, 1989, xxiv)

Attending to the popular in student experiences involves not simply valorizing that experience, but working with and on that experience. Such a pedagogy must allow students to speak from their own experience at the same time that it encourages them to identify and unravel the codes of popular culture that may work to construct subject relations that serve to silence and disempower them. Popular culture must be viewed as a complex and contradictory sphere in which dominant culture attempts to structure experience through the production of meaning, and which at the same time may provide possibilities for more open democratic formations.

The Media Schoolhouse

Theories of schooling have ignored the manner in which cultural institutions contain pedagogical practices that are as significant for learning as institutionalized education. As Philip Corrigan (1989, 79) notes, "we need to widen our understanding of how we are taught, and how we learn, and how we know," and this involves analyzing the pedagogy of popular culture forms.

Certainly, the dominant educational medium of contemporary culture is television, and the functioning of the pedagogical in this medium has a bearing on how education in general functions in our society. Elizabeth Ellsworth uses the concept of knowledge form—the level of organization of knowledge itself—in order to examine how educational media function to control knowledge. The pedagogy of the media must be examined according to a number of characteristics, including:

Organization of time and space, movement of encoded meanings at different rates of speed, definition of what counts as knowledge, assumptions about what goes on in the learning process, how it requires certain kinds of attention to what is happening, its norms of ambience and style, and its structuring of interpersonal relationships. (1989, 52)

Lawrence Grossberg (1989, 94) further demarcates the effective pedagogical terrain of popular culture, seeing it as operating at three levels: first,
the production of common sense—"the multilayered, fragmented collection
of meanings, values, and ideas that we both inherit and construct and which
largely define our taken-for-granted interpretations of the world. Second,
the determination of our libidinal and affective lives. Third, the production
of a site where our identities and experiences are constructed.

In the light of these concerns, television can be looked at as a pedagogical
machine, constructing discourses that function primarily in the locus of a
mode of transmission where "culture becomes defined solely by markets
for culture" (Wexler, 1989, 98). But the existence of television as an
instrument for blurring differentiated social discourses to the unifying sign
of the commodity should not be taken as the final victory of capitalism to
co-opt all oppositional discourses. Popular culture forms must be examined
as complex texts in context, which must be read dialectically. However, the
textual strategies of television, rooted in particular social institutions and
interests, privilege particular kinds of knowledge and particular forms of
pedagogical practice.

These become crucial questions for media education. We must examine
the extent to which the media themselves (as well as the influence of the
industry on our communication departments) influence how we conceive
of education and how the structure and practices of the media industries
influence our curriculum and models of pedagogy. Second, looking at media
as directly involved in cultural politics through a pedagogical moment will
lead us to define the object "media" in a different manner than does the
present atheoretical, depoliticized environment of the mass communication
department.

Teaching Media and Popular Culture

Finally, a critical pedagogy of media education must focus on the forms
of pedagogy used in teaching popular culture in the classroom. For critical
pedagogy this must be rooted in strategies of political struggle that recon-
struct schools as democratic public spheres. This involves both a language
of critique and a language of possibility (Giroux & McLaren, 1989, 130).
Radical educators have focused almost exclusively on ideological critique
to the detriment of drawing out the resistant and utopian possibilities in
popular culture forms. Critical pedagogy must instead both develop critical
literacy and draw out already existent counterhegemonic practices.

Giroux and Simon see critical literacy as a practice that legitimates "popular culture, cultural diversity, and dialogue as crucial elements in the debate about citizenship and cultural/social justice." They write:

If the question of literacy is linked to questions of purpose and meaning that take seriously the imperatives of educating students for critical citizenship in a mass society, it will have to be concerned with the issue of how students actually become self-reflective about the spheres of popular culture as part of the very process of learning. To be literate is not simply to know something; it also means knowing how to participate reflectively in the very act of producing knowledge. (1989, xi)

In examining popular culture, students must be led to ask whose interests are being served or challenged in a particular popular cultural practice, and what their own commitments are to those practices. Critical literacy as applied to the media is not simply a matter of reading off the ideologies of popular culture, but rather of seeing popular culture as "a field of practices that constitute for Foucault an indissoluble triad of knowledge, power and pleasure" (Giroux & Simon, 1989, 244). In practicing such a pedagogical struggle we consider what it is we have become, and what it is we no longer want to be. We also enable ourselves to recognize, and struggle for, possibilities not yet realized.

If we are to educate students to become media literate, we must attend to the multiple references and codes that position them. This means paying attention not only to the manner in which popular culture texts are constructed by and construct various discursive codes, but also how such texts express various contradictory ideological interests and how these texts might be taken up in a way that creates possibilities for different constructions of cultural and political life.

In a critical pedagogy of media education, the realm of practice—that is, the traditional areas of management, production and planning—would be integrated with the critical analysis of media. This is not a matter of reinforcing the schizophrenia we noted in the introduction, but rather bringing to bear a pedagogy as cultural politics on the sites of media education (TV studio 101), which have traditionally been left to professional, depoliticized approaches. On the other side, a sterile critical approach disconnected from media practice would consign the effects of media education to the academy. As Stanley Aronwitz states,

The point is that critical work without an effort to produce popular art forms remains a peculiarly intellectual take on cultural life which is already distant from the experience of students. What I am saying is this: There can be no cultural pedagogy without a cultural practice that both explores the possibilities of the form and brings out students' talents. (1989, 201)

CONCLUSION

We have seen how the neoconservative assault on education has defined a crisis that calls for both a return to a common high culture and a corresponding denigration of popular culture, and for a vocationalization of education, reducing it to little more than skills training for the market. This New Right vision of the future is actually a call to retrieve the past, and a mythic past, at that. The strategies of the neoconservatives are rooted in a conservative pedagogy that: (1) conceives of teaching as the transmission of neutral information; (2) calls for the elimination of the political from pedagogy while seeding all schooling with a hidden political agenda (especially by deriding multiculturalism and feminism); (3) works to silence student voice and to erase the everyday experience of work and popular culture from the educational environment; (4) reduces the tradition of democratic education (with its commitment to diversity, equality and justice) to providing equal chances to compete in the market; and (5) reduces the role of the intellectual to one of technician and patriot.

We have shown that critical pedagogy is a counterattack on this new hegemony of thinking in and about education and offers a proposal for a different practice that hopes for a better future. This future is one in which: (1) education serves in developing the ability of people to become active citizens, working toward a more radical democracy; (2) the concerns and experiences of diverse groups are addressed through dialogue; (3) theory and practice are integrated in developing practices of critical reflection and concrete action; and (4) the intellectual's functions become reconnected to the concrete concerns of the community and the nation, not through disinterested neutrality, but through moral and political action.

Our question is whose future will media education work toward? Our argument will be that the current direction of media education, although not always consciously, is in many ways already moving in line with the neoconservative project. The exact nature of media education's conservative direction will be examined in our analysis. By drawing upon critical pedagogy we will advance a critique of this direction and propose an alternative future. In the following chapter we will describe the theoretical developments in media studies, itself, offering a critique of the dominant trends in mass communication theory and pinpointing the critical concepts that will contribute to this redefinition of the purpose and goals of media education.

NOTES

1. A cultural studies that remains at the level of theory, particularly in analyzing the audience's response to media, ignores the extent to which production of media forms is set by commercial and governmental bodies. The political intervention into determining the scope and selection procedures of such granting bodies as the National Endowment for the Humanities, the National Endowment for the Arts, and so on—bodies that police the access to money for video and film production—is crucial to the furthering of a democratically motivated pedagogy. These organizations are under siege by the New Right, which hopes to channel them into overtly conservative political functions. Likewise, regulatory agencies, such as the Federal Communications Commission, are crucial sites for interventions by various media activist groups, if they hope to do more than simply offer critiques of the media.

2. This notion of "dissensus" refers to the phenomenon of the media's production of fragmentation and a multiplicity of voices that actively restricts democratic debate.

Chapter Two

Mass Communication Theory: Silence and Separation

> It is impossible to discuss communication or culture in our society without in the end coming to discussing power.
>
> Raymond Williams,
> "Communications and Community," 1961[1]

INTRODUCTION

Mass communication theory is built upon silence. While the idea of "mass communication" calls up images of collected voices gathered together (the continuous multitracked chorus of competing voices), mass communication theory produces little more than mute and wordless silence. In its travels through this century, the function of mass communication theory has somehow become one of dissection. It is the job of this theory (as theory turns back upon itself) to pull apart, separate and dissect these diverse and complex voices in order to reassemble them into the more manageable constructs (more marketable commodities) of media audiences and markets. This is theory built upon the silence of unasked questions, antecedent questions directed at the relations of power in the specific contexts of culture and history, which are essential to any meaningful analysis of the power of the mass media.

In many ways, then, this is a book about silence. In many ways, this is a book about separation—theory's separation from practice—and the deafening silence that results. A recent collection of essays on teaching communication (Daly, Friedrich & Vangelisti, 1990) offers us one representation of what David Lusted (1986, 3) decries as "the desperate undertheorization" of pedagogy. We are also offered insights into the character and operations of this stunted theory in the context of mass communication and media studies.

In his essay in that collection, "Teaching Mass Communication and Tele-communication," Thomas A. McCain offers us an unintentionally damning description of the state of mainstream mass communication theory:

The two issues that are central to understanding mass communication phenomena are the rather separate processes of encoding and decoding. Most courses and curricula need to address: (a) the processes and practices of organizations that produce, store, distribute, and transform information into mass communication messages and (b) the uses, consequences, or effects of this message content for individuals, groups, societies, and culture. Imbedded in both encoding and decoding processes is the problem of defining message content. A third issue, producing a theory that accounts for the encoding and decoding process in some kind of comprehensive fashion, is one of the elusive phenomena of mass communication, although there are several excellent summaries. (1990, 170)

We will begin by asking: What are the consequences of accepting an encoding/decoding model as a starting point? What are the consequences of accepting that these processes are best examined separately? How does one present a summary of that which still eludes us? If a metaphor of schizophrenia is useful in describing the present dilemma of the media educator, could the root cause of our affliction be this tradition of theory's denigration? Do similar separations result in similar silences throughout the traditions of mass communication theory, its practices and its history?

All mass communication is produced and consumed within institutional, social and cultural contexts. When media theory selects Lasswell's "Who says What to Whom through What channel with What effect?" as its starting point, even as it does so it ignores the complex and crucial power relations of "Who" to "Whom" and the entire cultural terrain on which they are played out. In this chapter we want to examine the emergence and institutionalization of mass communication theory within the greater institution of mass communication education in the United States. We hope to explore the promises contained in its initial emergence as a loosely collected and fragmented amalgam of questions and method that arose from the sweeping social and cultural changes in the United States of the late nineteenth and early twentieth centuries. We will also examine the problematic character of its (in many ways, superficial) coalescence into an academic field dominated by the hegemony of the quantitative social sciences.

THEORY'S TRAVELS THROUGH THE TWENTIETH CENTURY

Our earlier reference to Edward Said's notion of traveling theory was directed at its usefulness in placing emphasis upon the political context within which theory is developed and within which it is engaged with whatever practices it engenders. In some respects, mass communication theory begins its travels with the rise of Progressivism, as a social movement of the late nineteenth and early twentieth centuries. Progressivist thought coalesced around the effort to adjust to the loss of cultural continuity and the irrevocable altering of preindustrial constructions of community by the processes of industrialization, urbanization, new formations of mass culture (and the corresponding rise in literacy). The origins of contemporary mass communication theory may be traced to the earliest efforts of scholars in sociology, political science, psychology and related disciplines to understand these rapid reformations of a national culture.

The work of two leading progressivist thinkers, John Dewey (1859–1952) and Walter Lippmann (1889–1974), offers a glimpse of alternatives to the social-scientific approaches that would later rise to dominance in the theoretical development of mass communication. Lippmann's 1921 analysis of public opinion in the United States argued that the growing abilities of the mass media to maintain and reproduce dominant social inequalities, abilities manifest in its increasing skills in the affective naturalization of beliefs deeply grounded in cultural myth, represented a danger to democracy. Strongly predictive of the direction media theory would turn toward a half-century later,[2] the analysis seems to us now to stand as a road not taken; it offered a bridge connecting questions of the nascent mass media to the broader territories of a culture in a process of transformation.

A bridge was also envisioned between education and the role of the mass media in an ongoing project of social reconstruction. Dewey saw the emerging media as essential tools for a radical and emancipatory democracy. In his *The Public and Its Problems* (1927), the media were considered as the technological extension of a free press working toward the goals of social and political consensus through the broadest dissemination of the products of the increasingly sophisticated social sciences. More important, Dewey insisted that the social sciences should work to be conscious of the historical forces they exist within, and not arbitrarily separate facts from values. This separation of facts from values, a separation of quantity from quality, gave rise to an ideology of objectivity within a growing hegemony of quantitative social science. This should not, however, be read as an indictment of science and its influences upon media theory. Rather, these separations that have caused the stagnation of media theory also affect the sciences in ways suggested by Peters (1988), who argues that science, in general, ought to be "an act of imagining alternate ways of life or thought, a war on the actual in the name of the possible, [and that] science is not separate from but exemplary of the best intellectual practices" (309).

In examining the travels of early mass communication theory through the progressivist movement of the 1920s we also position theory at the historical juncture of the breakup of the traditional interdisciplinary university into the departmental structure, the identifying characteristic of the "modern" university. It is difficult to overstate the salience of theory's travel through these histories. In better understanding these moments, these transitions, we may better understand the manner in which the field of mass communication became entrenched in the constraints of professionalism and authority. Lastly, in better understanding this we may better understand also the potential contributions of critical pedagogy in extricating ourselves from this enervating theoretical problematic.

Media theory, in the form of a growing desire to understand the role of the emergent media in a greatly transformed cultural landscape, first appears in this period of transformation in the character of the university. Issues of legitimacy give rise to the corresponding desire to mark off disciplinary territories through the establishment of professional standards. The emerging importance of professionalism, increasingly positioned within the authority and neutrality of science, establishes an institutional ideology that continues to dominate our "common sense" understanding of higher education in the United States. The naturalization or "disappearance" of this particular set of institutional relations is the result of the loss of these moments to history. We would identify the recapture of this lost history, the reintegration or transformation of these moments into media theory (and the resultant impact of that reworked theory upon media practice) as central aspects of a project of critical media pedagogy.

MASS COMMUNICATION THEORY AND THE CHICAGO SCHOOL

Within these greater transformations of the university, the department of sociology at the University of Chicago introduced an approach to social theory directed at the importance of communication in social life, and employed ethnographic methods to explore the complex interrelationship of individual experience to the social context of that experience. The work of the Chicago School through the 1920s and 1930s offered a diverse, yet coherent and sustained image of the role of the mass media in the creation of a national culture. The growing disciplinary separations within the university and the resultant pressures for standards that would make the emerging divisions more visible, however, accelerated the move toward standard methods and to increasingly sophisticated statistical procedures. This was, in part, also embodied in a movement away from Chicago toward New York and Columbia University.

The steady rise of quantification, as the embodiment of professional legitimation in the cold objectivity of scientific knowledge, plays out across a complex and changing historical/cultural landscape. Charting media theory's travels through that landscape involves a host of elements. While a more complete treatment of any of these falls outside the scope of our purpose here, an understanding of media theory's position in relation to these diverse concurrent transformations is necessary for us to obtain a directional fix to chart these travels. To better locate theory's travels through this chapter we will attempt to sketch rough outlines of the more important elements while making reference to others.

The shift of influence from the broader and more expansive methods of the Chicago School to the scientific sociology of Columbia, while in keeping with the ascendency of objective scientific detachment, does not preclude its continuing influence reflected in developments in social phenomenology and social interaction approaches. Also critical to this portrait are the broader strokes of social and industrial development, the introduction of national brands and the rise of national marketing, increased sophistication in advertising, and the legitimation of applied psychology and the applied social sciences in general.[3] The application of social psychology to the mass media of the early 1930s and the resultant findings of the Payne Fund studies, that media effects are themselves mediated by a wide array of cross-influenced intervening variables, sound strikingly familiar a half-century later. Within this greater mural is the more focused and intentional movement of (far from unaffected) theory through the period of broadcasting's initial commercialization, and the salient shaping power of that period upon the corresponding developments (and decisions) in mass communication research.

THEORY AND THE IMPACT OF THE WORLD WARS

The development of mass communication theory/research was affected in many complex and interconnected ways by the events of World War II. As soldiers returned in the tens of thousands, rich with newly instituted educational benefits, the rapid postwar expansion of higher education in the

United States created a climate very supportive of the creation of new departments and programs.

This increasing trend toward separation, specialization and standardization created an overall sense of isolation and resulted in a growing tendency to look inward. Theory's development took an odd turn as research was increasingly directed at questions caught up with the state of knowledge within the researcher's own field rather than turned outward toward the larger questions of social and political conditions.

While we are not making an "evils of science" argument, this history of the political use of science by academics seeking the legitimation of disciplines and the establishment of departments is representative of theory's travels across intellectual and professional territories. We are arguing that the importance of these travels has become obscured across the intervening years. This loss of the perspective of historical context mystifies the relationship of theory to science, and further obscures the role of that relationship to the increased separation of theory's relationship to practice, that is, the depoliticization of theory. Jesse Delia (1987), in his history of communication research, also looks back at the phenomena of theory cut adrift from practice:

In retrospect, it is evident that this attitude to locate research problems within the matrix of disciplinary values rapidly entered communication research after WWII so for most researchers the commitment to science became detached from—and thereby made invisible—the commercial and political interests that had generated the basic research models in the first place. (58)

THEORY'S INWARD TURN

The separation of theory from practice occurred in this shift to a marked preference for the testing of theoretical hypotheses rather than a focus upon the social meaning and impact of public political communication. The separation of theory from practice was caught up in an understanding of a science that is free from values, leading social scientists to seek the authority of scientific objectivity and to turn toward "theory development" as a separate task within the theoretical environment of one's home discipline. This became the defining attitude for mainstream media research through the late 1950s and 1960s.[4]

Through the 1950s, the work of leading researchers such as Lazarsfeld, Berelson and Hovland continued to place a primary emphasis upon communication effects. By the end of the 1950s, mass communication theory had coalesced around a linear-effects perspective, with theory development as its principal project. The historically specific set of professional and commercial interests that underlay theory's initial organization, however, also served to restrict its future development. There is little surprising about the longevity of media effects as an area of interest and activity among communication researchers. Media effects seem a logical starting point, an area of obvious concern following both the initial introduction of these powerful new mass media, and the heightening of concerns raised during the world wars (World War II in particular) over their potential uses as mechanisms for social control.

It is also, however, in the effects literature itself that many of the theoretical limits and problems of quantitative analysis are best highlighted. Detached from any cultural moorings, the ability of these methods to connect the content and form of the mass media to their broader cultural context seems now to be ultimately confined to producing that summary now familiar to anyone who has ever passed through a mass communication theory/research methods course, that is, "Under some conditions some kinds of media will have some kinds of effects on some kinds of people some of the time" (representing precious little advance beyond the findings of the Payne Fund studies of the early 1930s).

Illustrating the limits of the methods, the effects literature also serves to illustrate the unavoidable political dimension of all research. Todd Gitlin (1978), in a landmark revisionist history/critique of the media effects literature, argues that the institutionalization of mass communication research, the separation of media theory from its own cultural practices, generated a body of administrative research in which the structures within which questions were originally phrased and asked was itself predisposed toward a certain understanding of broadcasting and the economic system within which it operated. This "dominant paradigm" of media theory and research, according to Gitlin, has

drained attention from the power of the media to define normal and abnormal social and political activity, to say what is politically real and legitimate and what is not; to justify the two-party political structure; to establish certain political agendas for social attention and to contain, channel, and exclude others; and to shape the images of opposition movements. . . . It has looked to the "effects" of broadcast programming in a specifically behaviorist fashion, defining "effects" so narrowly, microscopically, and directly as to make it very likely that survey studies could show only slight effects at most. . . . By studying only the "effects" that could be "measured" experimentally or in surveys, *it has put the methodological cart in front of the theoretical horse. Or, rather: it has procured a horse that could pull its particular cart.* (73–74, emphasis added)

By 1960 the basic components of this dominant paradigm (e.g., linearity of flow, short-term "measurable" effects) were well in place and representative of a superficially cohesive body of mainstream mass communication theory. The appearance of D. K. Berlo's *The Process of Communication* (1960) and Joseph Klapper's *The Effects of Mass Communication* (1960) also served to solidify this focus upon short-term media effects. Gitlin's analysis represents an important redirection of attention to the specific historical details of the emergence of this particular research model from the flurry of post–World War II research and its connections with the broader concerns of "the corporate interest of CBS and with the practical program of the Rockefeller Foundation and with the swelling positivist mode of American social science" (99). In other words, Gitlin's analysis does what critical analysis is supposed to do: it uses the lens of history to refocus our contemporary understanding of the naturalized underpinnings of media theory and practice (i.e., to "make the invisible visible"), and in particular, the historical conditions in which theory's separation from practice occurred.

USES AND GRATIFICATIONS

Of the various research strategies to emerge from post–World War II mass communication literature, uses and gratifications (or "media gratifications") proved to be a lasting blend of sociological functionalism and media effects approaches, repositioned in the context of Robert Merton's (1957/67, 39) notion of "theories of the middle range." A summary of the origins and underpinnings of uses and gratifications theory is offered by Dennis McQuail (1984), for whom its initial motives included

a simple wish to know more about the audience; an awareness of the importance of individual differences in accounting for the audience experience; a still fresh wonderment at the power of popular media to hold and involve their audiences; and an attachment to the case study as an appropriate tool and an aid to psychological modes of explanation. (177)

Represented by a body of literature with origins in studies conducted in the 1940s, uses and gratifications evolved as an empirically bountiful approach (a reference to its functionalist beginnings) from which to examine the relationship between the mass media and its audiences. Its search for functions served by media consumption generated an expansive literature of slightly modified media effects studies, each focused upon some small context of media/audience interaction to the exclusion of all other factors.

Following a period of inactivity in the 1950s and early 1960s, the publication of *The Uses of Mass Communications* (Blumler & Katz, 1974) signaled a revitalization and subsequent rearticulation of uses and gratifications theory. This took the form of a now classic seven-point outline in which the uses and gratifications theory was described as expressing a concern with:

(1) the social and psychological origins of (2) needs which generate (3) expectations of (4) the mass media or other sources, which lead to (5) differential patterns of media exposure (or engagement in other activities), resulting in (6) need gratifications and (7) other consequences, perhaps mostly unintended ones. (Katz, Blumler & Gurevitch, 1974, 20)

In the following decade, a shift occurred within the uses and gratifications literature away from its position as middle-range theory toward the more ambitious goal of field-defining research paradigm. In their analysis of uses and gratifications studies of the 1970s and early 1980s, Phillip Palmgreen, Lawrence Wenner and Karl Rosengren (1985) identified eight linked assumptions, expanding the scope of uses and gratifications theory:

(1) the audience is active, thus (2) much media use can be conceived as goal directed, and (3) competing with other sources of need satisfaction, so that when (4) substantial audience initiative links needs to media choice, (5) media consumption can fulfill a wide range of gratifications, although (6) media content alone cannot be used to predict patterns of gratifications accurately because (7) media characteristics structure the degree to which needs may be gratified at different times, and, further, because (8) gratifications obtained can have their origins in media content, exposure in and of itself, and/or the social situation in which exposure takes place. *These assumptions hold in a climate in which judgments about the cultural significance of media are suspended.* (14, emphasis added)

This blanket removal of cultural concerns from uses and gratification's theoretical equation works to reproduce further the separation of media researchers from political commitment and self-reflection, while failing to add to the ability of its collective literature to move beyond the "for some people, under some conditions . . . " qualifications.

Media theory and research operate within a framework of society and culture greater than any single theory or research method could ever hope to accommodate. The theoretical difficulties of uses and gratifications theory point to the inevitable failure of any theory that attempts to understand or explain the mass media and the media audiences in isolation, bracketed off from their greater cultural location.

SILENCES AND SEPARATIONS

Theory's travels through this odd historical combination of moments led to the idea of mass communication theory that appeared as the primary guiding and organizing force in the 1960s. Both the scholarly and academic traditions (they are sometimes the same, sometimes not) of mass communication in the United States emerged within this complex political economy of broadcasting and advertising set within the drama of two world wars. Within this greater historical narrative the nascent social sciences struggled for legitimation, adopting, adapting and affecting the signs and symbols of the natural sciences, seeking to dress themselves in the detached authority of scientific knowledge.

During this period, theory's development was accelerated through the focused interests of both the military and big business. The influences of a militaristic capitalism often seem to rest just beneath the surface of summaries of mass communication theory, rising to the surface in the focused importance of control in the hands of the message producer in the communication process. For example, in the introduction to a standard mass communication theory text, a set of assumptions seem to underlie the way in which the power relations implicit in mass communication are presented:

Communication theory is aimed at improving our understanding of the process of mass communication. With better understanding, we are in a better position to predict and control the outcomes of mass communication efforts. The act of communication can be observed from a number of points of view, but two of the most important are that of the source (or media practitioner), and that of the receiver (or mass communication audience). (Severn & Tankard, 1992, 4)

In its contemporary (modern and postmodern) meaning and usage, the audience is the creation/invention/innovation of a Post–World War I political economy out of which radio emerged as a national advertising medium.

This complex intertwining set of elements, woven together across the past seventy years, can seem at times to resemble an expansive big-screen Hollywood narrative. The plot: The emerging broadcast communications industries provide funding for research which, in the process, draws attention to those questions that best serve its needs. The presence of industry money (and the potential for more) plays a significant role in the emergence of departments and schools of mass communication (radio/television, media arts, telecommunications, etc.). These investments, and the rapid concurrent explosion of media into new markets via corresponding explosions in satellite and computer technologies throughout the 1960s and 1970s, also have significant impact in the shaping of the undergraduate media curriculum.

Our cast is peppered with an endless procession of walk-ons (speaking parts, unfortunately) by "industry people" in semiretirement in faculty positions. Usually teaching courses offered under the umbrella term of "communication management," they bring, to otherwise academic departments, bottom-line "real world" experience. This often serves to exacerbate furiously the dichotomy of "ivory tower" versus "real world" (or, the classroom-general-theoretical versus the workplace-specific-practical) that plagues contemporary undergraduate media education. These parts, while minor, help move the story forward toward a major plot point: the movement of mass communication from schools and colleges of liberal arts and humanities into professional schools (and the continued separation of media theory from its practice).

The effects tradition grounded mass communication theory in three elements: the media industry (whose contribution was to direct research interest toward a certain understanding of audience and toward questions of what that audience consumes and why); the military (whose interests in the uses of mass communication as a means of social control mirrored, in many ways, the interests of advertisers); and functionalism. While functionalism has a noted tendency to collapse under theoretical critique, these three elements worked to close off the space from which such a critique could arise. In the context of practice separated from theory, functionalism blossomed as a fruitful practice, rich with limitless variations of short-term effects studies, each discrete and separate from the next.

MEDIA THEORY, CULTURE AND NEW TECHNOLOGY

Major advancements in technology, especially in the area of computers, also played across these three elements in important ways. The increased articulation and refinement provided to statistically based quantitative methods further strengthened the dominance of functionalism. Advertising and marketing made concurrent advancements in their ability to construct increasingly elaborate demographic and psychographic portraits of media audiences. More directly, these technologies led to tremendous advancements in the techniques of film and video production, creating a cottage industry in computer-driven special effects that increasingly amaze, stun and narcotize entertainment audiences (while blurring the distinctions between news, entertainment and advertising).

Finally, it was as if all aspects of these computer/communication technologies came together in the celebration of "smart" technology in the Gulf

War. The Gulf War seems an impossibly thick and complex subject for analysis, certainly exceeding the scope of this chapter. However, it represents a culminating marriage of all the elements that have been caught up in this description of theory's travels.

Throughout the war's brief history, technology seemed to make all things possible. The weaponry seemed numbingly accurate as it transmitted images of its own destruction. The news coverage became a church to that technology, ignoring its flaws and limits, the deaths by "friendly fire" and six-figure casualty counts, which would challenge those impressions of clean, efficient accuracy. Though brief, the war spilled over into all aspects of U.S. popular culture. All the contradictions, tensions and unresolved conflict that constitute the American character boiled to the surface in the form of posterized slo-mo "news" footage, t-shirts and bumper stickers, and *Terminator II*, the most expensive film of all time (the perfect marriage of technology and marketing), in which the hero is "smart" technology/weaponry. The film's star, Arnold Schwarzenegger, a highly visible Reagan/Bush Republican, became, in a fever of "news" coverage, the first civilian to purchase the military's new all-terrain transport vehicle (the "hum-vee") for personal use.[5] Boiling over into the form of jokes told in bars and crudely drawn cartoons, the war brought to the surface all the cultural undercurrents of an unholy trinity of sexism, homophobia and racism.[6]

This continuing acritical and undertheorized emphasis upon communication technology has become increasingly problematic in models of "learning technologies" or "integrated technologies" developed by universities and representative of efforts often couched in terms of "trying to bring education into the next century." These efforts appear to us as fundamentally conservative in their presentation of technology as beneficial by definition of its ability better to support current social structures, thus enabling them to function more efficiently. We see nowhere in the discourse of new technology any place for the open discussion of an ideology of technology.

While in many important respects reactionary, new communication/media technologies are positioned as progressive by virtue of their role as signifiers of progress within the modernist tradition. Under these conditions, silence erupts as language recedes in its very capacity for expression. As theory is cut adrift from practice, words like "critical" and "progressive" are cut adrift from their underlying political meanings. Within this context, critical assessments of technology (or even the expression of reservations regarding its acritical applications) are in constant danger of being positioned as representing conservative, that is, antichange, attitudes. The critic is in danger of being marginalized as an old curmudgeon, an eccentric iconoclast unable to accept or adapt to the bright new world. Theory, cut off from practice, is silent. And it is only in the relocation of the terms of this discussion into the greater context of culture that these questions can be approached.

RECENT QUESTIONS AND THE VOICES OF CULTURE

Throughout this charting of theory's travels through the twentieth century, our emphasis has been upon the causes underlying its slow separation from its origins in critical examinations of media's role in social/cultural transformations, examinations that regularly employed historical, critical and ethnographic methods of data collection and analysis.The historical separation of media theory from media practice involved a process of compartmentalization in which questions about the relationship of media to the greater social structures within which it exists were systematically broken up in to small pieces, separated by method, separated by question and content, separated by theoretical approach. One result of these territorial divisions was the separate evolution of film studies and popular culture studies independent of communication research. With little exception, the mass culture debates of the 1950s took place outside the territory of mass communication as it had marked its boundaries.

Separated by program, department, school and college, the study of communication fragmented into divisions of rhetoric, speech, interpersonal and mass communication (itself distinct and separate from journalism).[7] These separations (sometimes more influenced by power struggles within the bureaucratic structures of the university than by theoretical debates) spilled over into the structures of graduate programs, were reinforced, and eventually reproduced again into undergraduate curricula.[8] These separations also reverberate in the academic/scholarly literatures, where boundaries and territories are clearly marked by conferences and journals, theory and method.

By locating this project in the greater projects of cultural studies and critical pedagogy, we suggest a path out of the silence of these separations, a path toward a reunification of theory with its practice, toward a critical media pedagogy historically conscious of (and not blindly driven by) the structures of power within which it is integrated. It is a path, however, resisted in the deepest structures of the contemporary university, resisted in the profound ways in which these practices of separation and silence are emphasized, reproduced and maintained.

This project of reunification is made more difficult by critical theory's insistence that what is necessary is far more than the simple collaboration of scholars from various humanities disciplines, each making a contribution to the larger project from the relative safety of his or her own discipline.

Recalling the debates in the early days of the Centre for Cultural Studies in Birmingham, Stuart Hall notes:

What we discovered is that serious interdisciplinary work does not mean that one puts up the interdisciplinary flag and then has a kind of coalition of colleagues from different departments, each of whom brings his or her own specialization to a kind of academic smorgasbord from which students can sample each of these riches in turn. Serious interdisciplinary work involves the intellectual risk of saying to professional sociologists that what they say sociology is, is not what it is. . . . It was *never a question of which disciplines would contribute to the development of this field, but of how one could decenter or destabilize a series of interdisciplinary fields.* (Hall, 1990, 16, emphasis added)

By the late 1970s the problems underlying the dominant approach to mass communication research and theory development were boiling over into the mainstream literature. *Ferment in the Field*, a special issue of the *Journal of Communication* (1983), marked the start of a decade of extended debate and discussion over theory and method. It also helped to identify the way media theory development was impeded by the denigration of historical and cultural methods and by a standing practice of ignoring European critical research (part of the general rejection of nonstatistical approaches to communication phenomena). These debates, however, failed to come to terms with the issue of teleology. Are our efforts directed toward a paradigm or "grand theory" capable of, in some presently unimaginable fashion, bringing together the broad and diverse collection of concepts, approaches, methods, theoretical orientations, and so on that now seems to represent our current understanding of media studies as a field? Just what exactly (or even inexactly) does this notion of "bringing together" really mean?

The concept of paradigm is grounded in the historically based need of a given academic area to establish itself, both intellectually and bureaucratically, as a coherent area of knowledge with the capacity to understand some complex and significant (i.e., large) phenomena in some complex and large way. Mainstream communication research continues, by and large (in mainstream journals, at national professional meetings, in graduate programs, etc.), on the path of self-directed research aimed at continued theory development in a climate of continued isolation (within a self-contained universe a paradigm may seem a more plausible proposition). Some argue (Nelson, 1985) that communication is inherently antiparadigmatic, situationally bound, constant only in its shape-shifting character. Others, less convinced this early in its development, suggest that the field "is not intellectually stagnant; it is confused. It, like many fields in the late twentieth century . . . does not know what it means when it talks about itself as a field or discipline" (Peters, 1988, 316).

The important point in our analysis involves the indivisible nature of the relationships among elements and practices systematically (and historically) separated out. It is in this context that the study of media and mass communication is understood as the study of culture. Stuart Hall reminds us that, in this context, the theory of culture is defined as

the study of relationships between elements in a whole way of life. "Culture" is not a practice; nor is it simply the descriptive sum of the "mores and folkways" of societies—as it tended to become in certain kinds of anthropology. It is threaded through all social practices, and is the sum of their inter-relationship. (Hall, 1980, 60)

The study of media must be reintegrated into the greater study of culture in order to begin to understand both itself and its object(s) of study as complex sets of social and cultural formations and practices. The oppositional dichotomy of quantitative/"administrative" versus qualitative/"critical" research traditions may be less the result of intrinsic political stances interwoven throughout each perspective, than the direct result of this history of separations arising from theory's rendering from practice, and out of which these political oppositions have arisen. Finally, perhaps, the problem with media theory is the problem of restricting the focus of theory to that of the media. The tradition of mainstream mass communication research is a tradition built upon a foundation of silence (problematic, but unproblematized). It is a tradition that seeks to study the power of the media (hence, the prolonged emphasis upon effects) while avoiding fundamental antecedent questions about power. It is a tradition that has produced what might be referred to as theory's great qualifier, "for some people, under some conditions, some of the time, some effects." Media theory's reunification with the cultural conditions of its forms and practices holds the possibility that the underlying questions of power (the missing element in the equation that produces these relations among people, conditions and history) examined across a broader cultural terrain might produce a more sophisticated understanding of the "power of the mass media."

This reconnecting of the study of media to its cultural moorings is not, in itself, sufficient to reconnect the study of media (theory) to the role played by media in the greater/political struggle for equality and fairness. The dominant construction of cultural studies in the United States today is based upon the cultural theory of the Birmingham School. However, in that transatlantic adaptation the roots of the British project in adult education were somehow lost. While an important element in our project involves expanding the scope of mass communication theory into a media studies cognizant of its role within a field of cultural relations, the reintegration of theory and practice can best be accomplished through finding the means to connect media theory to media practice in the context of media education.

A metaphor of building bridges is central to what we want to do. The building of bridges must occur between two literatures, two theoretical traditions: mass communication and critical pedagogy. Through this bridging we may bring about the disruption of that set of distancing dichotomies that have engendered this historical climate of silence and separation. This does not involve the simple bringing of critical scholarship into the media classroom and the increase of theory and criticism courses in the curriculum. Rather, it entails the more difficult and unsettling task of breaking down (or bridging) the distances between teacher and student, between teaching and research, and between the library and the street. These distances, once crossed, can open new spaces from within which traditionally silenced voices might speak. These distances cut off the discourse of a pedagogical practice out of which new theory can emerge. We now turn our attention toward the current theory and practice of media education in the contemporary university.

NOTES

1. "Communications and Community" is the text of the William F. Harvey Memorial Lecture, given at Bedford College, University of London, on April 8, 1961. It is published in the posthumously assembled book *Resources of Hope* (Williams, 1989).

2. This also seems predictive of the success of the Willie Horton prison furlough ads of the 1988 U.S. presidential campaign.

3. The world wars were crucial in the advancement of applied psychology as a major player in support of the military's recruitment and personnel selection and management functions. The contributions of applied psychologists to the war effort during World War II completed the process of legitimation that had worked its way out across the first half of the century.

4. Delia (1987, 61) details this movement toward a grand organizing paradigm within communication research as facilitated by three factors: (1) the adoption of a vocabulary of organizing terms, (2) the establishment of a core subject matter with the appearance of field-defining books, and (3) the embracing of a standard conception of the "basic communication approach."

5. David Tetzlaff has described to the authors the difference between the two *Terminator* films as the "difference between pre– and post–Gulf War America."

6. Many cartoons depicted stereotyped and caricatured Arabs (often Saddam Hussein) being made to endure the humiliation of forced homosexual sex at the

hands of U.S. soldiers, George Bush or Uncle Sam. A joke typical of the period was "What do you call two Iraqi women coming into a bar? Incoming scuds."

7. These separations follow those of the nineteenth century, in which the intellectual pursuit of knowledge was fragmented into the separate areas of English, history, religion, and so on.

8. In our experience, and the experiences of numerous friends and colleagues, it seems far too common that mass communication and interpersonal/speech communication doctoral students rarely interact.

Part Two:

The Structural Problematic of Media Education

Chapter Three

The Conditions of Media
Education Practice

In order to understand the theoretical and practical implications of media education, we need first to take an empirical and historical look at media education in the universities. It should be clear that the way communication and media departments function is not an isolated phenomenon. It reflects a general problem in education and it reflects a system one would expect in an advanced capitalist society. The primary problem is that education is conceived as a commodity that is purchased for its use-value in procuring employment. Further, education functions in this exchange as a means of disciplining and channeling students to take up functions in industry and commerce in a manner in which they conceptualize the media itself as a commodity.

The actual situation is not as simple as this general statement makes it appear; we need to analyze the specific historical factors around which media education congealed and we need to understand the particular structuring of media departments in their empirical specificity. We will examine the rise in popularity of media education and its historical development. Then we will look at the current structure of media departments: their departmental definitions, curricula and place within the university. We will then connect the various empirical findings with the theoretical concerns laid out in the previous two chapters.

THE HISTORY OF MEDIA EDUCATION IN AMERICAN
UNIVERSITIES

We do not intend to present a comprehensive history of media education, but rather to focus on a number of factors that have led to the contemporary trends in departments that focus on mass communication. Thus, we will not deal in detail with the history of theoretical and research traditions that led to the defining of the disciplines of communication, mass communication and journalism education, nor will we focus on the cross-fertilizations of rhetoric and speech with media curricula, or the peculiar development of midwestern doctoral programs (a phenomenon that would require an account of the influence of schools of social science, connections to policy and marketing and individual efforts to forge a definite discipline of mass communication research). These concerns would take us far afield from our specific intentions, which are to describe the current approaches to undergraduate education within departments of media, mass communication and communication arts.

This being said, we do need to attend to some initial factors in the rise of communication as a discipline. The study of communication and media arose primarily through the efforts of high-level scholarship in the disciplines of social psychology, sociology and political science. This established the prominence of social science techniques and empirical research in American mass communication research and also established the interdisciplinary nature of the field. It was not until the early 1940s that specific departments of mass communication arose; these were predominantly defined as graduate educational departments. At the same time as empirical work developed on public opinion, propaganda and mass media, cultural and literary approaches began to develop within departments of English and to a lesser extent theater, history and art. This work primarily focused on film, due to its artistic pretensions and its reworking of the form of the novel. Thus, film study developed as a separate discipline and established its own departments, organizations and scholarly journals.

One should not underestimate the significance of this peculiar situation— the division between mass communication (dealing with mass media such as television and radio conceived in terms of their social and social psychological effects) and film (dealing with aesthetic, phenomenological and cultural processes embodied in film "texts"). This division accounts, in part, for the specific nature of media departments with their industrial design approach versus the aesthetic focus of film practice programs. (There are industrial programs in film, centered in Hollywood and New York, but the aesthetic and creative credentials of graduates such as Spike Lee and Martin Scorsese attest to the artistic emphasis even within these predominantly "factory" schools.) The point here is that the American conception of theoretical and empirical work in mass communication defined the approaches toward media education in a direction that excluded broader concerns with art, aesthetics, textuality, cultural processes and the production of meaning.

In a sense the industrial, practical, professional approach that has developed in media education is the other side of the social science orientation of advanced media research. However, this is not the whole story. In the past 20 years, media education has seen an influx of critical approaches that made some impact on the field. Although, in the United States, the dominant empirical paradigm stills holds sway, the approaches of cultural studies have acquired their own foothold. As we will see, this has yet to have a strong effect on undergraduate education in mass communication, where professionalism and industry approaches predominate.

Most people working on mass media phenomenon in the 1920s would not have conceived of a separate discipline known as mass communication. They were working in established disciplines, using the techniques and theories of social science and applying them to media and mass social phenomena. Even when the field of mass communication coalesced in the 1940s its interdisciplinarity was still predominant in practice. Despite this, institutional and professional forces pushed the formation of a "discipline" forward. There are still those who see the study of mass communication as a specific and concrete discipline, with an object, specific methodologies and theories. This disciplinary impetus persists, despite the fact that the field has no real coherence: its object—the mass media—is simultaneously a text, effect, practice, outcome, structure, and so on; its methodologies are borrowed from social science in general; its theories, such as they are, are reworkings of social and psychological theories or else circular models centered around undeveloped models of information and "communication." The question remains, why did mass communication evolve into a discipline despite these shortcomings, despite this interdisciplinary history?

The reason, we believe, lies in its "other" history, as a practical field with industry connections and professional training goals. Even the "pure science" of the mass communication researchers betrayed this influence—their research, dependent on large grants to conduct experiments and surveys, required practical connections to marketing and policy functionaries. One need look no further than the namesakes of various schools of mass communication and journalism to see this influence (the Scripps-Howard School of Journalism, the Pulitzer School, the Newhouse School, etc.). Even in the early part of the century, the need for professional practitioners to be trained in industry techniques within a general college education was recognized (journalism education dates from 1903; by 1930 there were 455 schools offering journalism courses). As the media became a mega-industry this need increased, and colleges answered the need. Today, more and more media professionals have acquired their initial training in the universities.

Broadcasting education dates from the 1930s, when colleges offered courses in radio through departments of fine art, music or business administration. The first professionally oriented department dates from 1939. By the late 1940s there were about 75 universities and colleges offering degrees in broadcasting. The bulk of these degrees were offered through speech and theater departments or journalism departments. By 1960 there were 89 schools offering broadcasting degrees, and as the demand increased the need for separate programs in broadcasting and mass communication was recognized. In the 1960s and 1970s the trend toward separate professional programs in broadcasting entered full swing—47 departments of broadcasting came into existence. The largest trend, however, was toward the formation of "communication" departments that offered several different major tracks such as public relations, advertising, broadcasting, speech, rhetoric, and so forth; 77 such departments existed by 1972 (Katzen, 1975).

Today this trend has continued. From 1976 to 1988, the number of undergraduates enrolled in mass communication increased by approximately 32 percent and by 1988, 147,000 students were enrolled in journalism and mass communication programs (Becker, 1989, 3). This incredible growth in the popularity of the field is explained by a number of factors: the growth of the television and cable industries and the corresponding growth in employment opportunities in these fields; the presentation in mass media of the high status and high salary nature of the media profession; the trend toward a service—"information"—society; and the tendency of students increasingly to define their college education in terms of future employment. Around the country, communication is seen by students as a discipline that offers the opportunity for future employment in an exciting field.

As we have noted, the history of the connection between university education in communication and the media industry goes back to the initial research ventures in marketing and propaganda, where funding for projects determined an instrumental, administrative orientation in mass communication research. In addition, since World War II, the broadcast industry has been increasingly seeking college graduates for employment. The media industries have not been active in developing their own training mechanisms and have relied more and more on universities to provide "raw" talent. Universities and colleges, recognizing the growth in the media fields, have been active in establishing industry tie-ins through professional organizations such as the Broadcast Education Association (BEA) and the National Association of Broadcasters (NAB);[1] internship programs; training facilities such as semiprofessional and professional radio and cable outlets;

boards of advisees composed of local broadcast executives; and, to a lesser extent, direct funding of facilities by media industry individuals and corporations. In addition, the lack of graduate departments early on meant that faculty in broadcasting were drawn from industry. The structuring of departments of communication in their advent was defined by this professional faculty who were rooted in industry procedures and practices.

Further, communication has always occupied a precarious position in the university structure—is it a humanity, an art, a social science, a profession? The relative newness of media education in comparison to the traditional disciplines has put it in a position where the field must justify itself. Given the tenuous nature of the discipline as a field of intellectual endeavor (is its object worthy of study?) in the eyes of the other disciplines, media education has tended toward justifying its existence in terms of occupational relevance. It is a money maker for the university.

Finally, the growth in professionalism and industry connections as defining the nature of broadcast education is, in part, due to increasing attention to the so-called information revolution. Social scientists, government sources and popular media have all jumped on the bandwagon of info-revolution discourse and have called for increased use of high technology in all sectors of the economy. Communication programs have recognized these trends and have accordingly steered their resources toward tie-ins with industrial information use. Many department descriptions now begin with a statement about the need for students to get on the information revolution bandwagon.

This brief history of media education has pointed out a number of factors that have led the field to define itself as professionally oriented, technologically advanced and employment-motivated. Obviously, not all of the factors involved in the history of media education have been covered, nor have other alternative developments (in cultural studies programs or comparative and international communication programs, for example) been described. Also, it is obvious that the development of media education could have gone in another direction; there is nothing natural in this development. Part of our project is to deconstruct this history in order to open possibilities for other directions for the field. In order to accomplish this goal, we must take a closer, critical look at the contemporary structure of media education in the university setting.

THE STRUCTURE OF DEPARTMENTS AND CURRICULA

Currently, there are approximately 100,000 students enrolled in 600 departments with 2,000 faculty that in some manner define themselves as within the media discipline (these figures do not include print journalism departments or departments of communication without any mass communication area). How these departments define themselves is evidence of a variety of administrative decisions and of the tenuous nature of the field. For example, in a survey of schools offering undergraduate degrees with course work in mass media, we found the following departmental designations: Communication(s), Communication Arts, Communication Arts and Sciences, Communication Studies, Communication(s) Media, Mass Communication, Journalism and Mass Communication, Speech Communication, Telecommunication(s), Radio/Television, Media Arts, Broadcasting, Broadcast Communication Arts and Journalism-Broadcasting. This plethora of titles testifies not to the diversity of approaches to the field but rather to the extent to which the study of the media has found a home in a number of administrative units due to its popularity and seeming fit with given departmental structures. Department of Communication seems to be the most popular title currently. The most common structure of such departments includes divisions of mass communication and speech communication (additionally, departments may contain divisions of speech pathology, theater, broadcasting, public relations, journalism or rhetoric).

According to data gathered by Limberg (1987), the orientation of administrative units in media education are predominantly in liberal arts (69%) or professional (22%) divisions. Our survey showed no real difference in the orientation of department curricula whether they were defined as liberal arts or professional. The orientation of programs toward training and professional occupational education seemed not to depend on where they were located in the university. Approximately 85 percent of the programs took a professionally oriented approach, as defined by fulfilling most (if not all) of the following criteria: (1) percentage of course work in broadcast training, (2) percentage of course work in management training, (3) direct statements of occupational outcomes, such as "prepares students for careers in . . ." (this specific phrase occurred in 25 out of 75 catalog statements examined), (4) internship programs, (5) professional accreditation, (6) investment in technology, (7) tracks defined in terms of occupational goals (broadcast, broadcast journalism, public relations and advertising, management, engineering, production, etc.).

This professional orientation is further documented in the course curricula of the departments. Warner and Liu (1990) showed that the most popular sequences in media departments were broadcast news, TV production and management. Sequences in criticism, writing and mass communication study were offered by only 3 percent of the schools, topped even by sequences in sales and broadcast performance. Although many curriculum descriptions in our survey referred to "a liberal arts orientation," "general education," or "critical thinking," the actual balance of courses in these departments was skewed at least two to one in favor of professional career preparation courses such as broadcast announcing, journalistic writing or TV/audio production.

Our survey examined a range of overall institutional settings: small liberal arts schools, private general universities, private research universities, specialized institutes (Emerson, for example), community colleges, state satellite colleges and universities, elite state universities and large state research universities. As would be expected, the smaller private institutions tended to have smaller and more specialized departments, some of which focused on general critical orientations. The larger private institutions were more focused on professional training, although some research universities emphasized theory and research at the graduate level. The specialized institutes and community colleges were wholly vocational in orientation. State satellite schools tended to be large departments with heavy emphasis on production and management, whereas the elite state schools had more balanced programs (although still structured in sequences defined by career tracks). The large state research schools varied, sometimes emphasizing general education, while obviously aimed primarily at graduate education.

Overall, there is a consistency in media education that is characterized by a dominant professional training orientation, motivated, in part, by attracting students to the field through its occupational promises. This orientation is, of course, rooted in a number of practicalities, such as the need to keep enrollments up, the general trend in college education toward career advancement and the pressure from legislators, parents and industry to provide "productive" and "efficient" schooling that prepares students to contribute to society in an instrumental fashion. What we would like to propose is that the goals of media education in this direction are not necessarily the ones we should have and, even more significantly, that the professional orientation of the schools does not necessarily fulfill its promise. We will now attempt to evaluate critically the current structure and orientation of media education. We will connect this analysis with some of the concepts of critical pedagogy and critical media theory that we have laid out in the previous two chapters.

A CRITIQUE OF MEDIA EDUCATION STRUCTURE

University education as it has evolved generally stresses two predominant goals that interconnect and support each other (we will discuss the particulars of liberal education and critique it as a fully adequate model in the next chapter): the general education of the individual, divorced from the narrow specialization of vocational goals, and the development of specific skills and mastery of particular knowledges that lead to productive employment. One of the purposes of liberal education is to develop students' general intellectual abilities in order to provide them with the knowledge and skills they need to be active citizens in a democracy. Second, liberal education aims to educate the student to become expert in a field, through providing specific disciplinary focus in a field of endeavor, that is nevertheless presented in the context of a general knowledge base. Thus, liberal education does provide vocational direction, but not within a conception of a narrow professionalism disconnected from the wider purposes of a liberal education. As the Association for Education in Journalism and Mass Communication (AEJMC) Liberal Arts and Sciences Task Force puts it: "A liberal arts education equips students to be practical as well as creative problem solvers. A knowledge of the ways human beings and their institutions have tried to describe and explain the world and respond to its opportunities and emergencies is at the heart of the principle of the 'educated person' " (1989, 9).

It would be absurd to claim that university education is or should be disconnected from the purposes of providing students with a level of education that leads to some kind of fruitful employment, but such an emphasis does not require a purely technical focus on discrete job skills in rigidly defined occupational slots. We need to examine how media education within communication departments squares with these goals. How has it defined itself in terms of the goals of liberal education and vocational training?

The Discourse of Professionalism

Our description of the rise of media education has drawn attention to the professionalization of educational objectives in the field. We need to define what this professional approach is and how it has diverged from the goals of liberal education set out above. The evidence for our account will be drawn from personal experience (the authors have direct working experience in a total of eight departments as well as familiarity with twenty other departmental operations), syllabi and curricular statements from a sample of departments, and articles on pedagogy drawn from the literature of various professional organizations in the field.

What is the professional approach? A professional education in the media can be defined as one that attempts to prepare students for entry-level jobs in the commercial mass media or corporate communication industries by replicating professional techniques and procedures in the classroom. In media production this involves training in equipment techniques and program formats currently employed in the industry. In media journalism it involves practice in replicating the form of broadcast copy under a structure of strict deadlines. In media management and law it involves simulations of broadcast decision-making and legal procedure, often through the use of computer programs that incorporate industry data and practices.

How are departments structured in terms of this professional approach to education? First, the majority of departments attempt to introduce the student to the field through a core curriculum that usually includes a basic survey course, an introductory writing course, a basic production course (audio/video) and sometimes a media and society course (Warner & Liu, 1990). After a basic introduction to the field, students are usually tracked into sequences according to their vocational interest—production, management, journalism, advertising/public relations, law and policy. The introductory core usually introduces the student to basic history, theory and methodology in the field, as well as rudimentary consideration of criticism and social effects. These core elements are nowhere expanded in the sequences that follow. In addition, the approach to the introduction of the field is often conducted in a general pro-industry ethos (celebration of media achievements and personalities, guest lectures by successful broadcasters, technological marvels, etc.). As a result, students are generally led to perceive the critical and theoretical content of these courses as required for advancement to the "real" meat of the major, and treat them as a hurdle to be gotten over.

This introduction to the field sets up the expectations of the student in the direction of vocational choices that will be the real content of their education. Although a majority of departments pay lip service to the goals of liberal education, the actual practice is to separate systematically liberal and professional education, in a direction that subordinates the former to the latter. This professionalization of media education is evident in the discourse of departmental goal statements and in the educational literature of the field.

Contemporary debate in the discourse of media pedagogy centers around the value of a liberal arts approach versus a professional approach to media studies. Although many scholars in the field have expressed a concern with an overemphasis on professionalism, this concern is only beginning to have its effects on pedagogy. We still find an overwhelming tendency toward professionalism and vocationalism. This is expressed in departmental mission statements, which usually begin with a statement of the wish to "blend theory and practice," or that "all majors are expected to develop sound theoretical knowledge and practical skills," or that "our program is founded in a sound education in liberal arts." The curriculum of the departments from which these statements were gleaned, however, show a ratio of three or four to one in favor of professionally oriented courses. There are a number of possible interpretations of this contradiction: (1) the curriculum statements are written to please the administration or other interests in the university, not to describe the department; (2) the liberal arts portion of the educational experience is actually left to other university departments; (3) the statements express an actual desire for the stated goal, but in reality the practice of training students for jobs relegates the liberal education goal to secondary status.

In addition to departments that attempt, however unsuccessfully, to meld liberal and professional education there are many (approximately 60%) that state their objectives as wholeheartedly vocational. Here we see statements such as "mass media studies is designed for students who wish to prepare for careers," "the major appeals to students who wish to pursue creative careers," or "the program provides training for professional work." In fact, our survey of curricular mission statements showed that 93 percent of the schools referred to preparation for careers, jobs, occupations or professional work as one of their major objectives.

The actual practices of these departments (as opposed to their discourse) is another question. Here, the overwhelming evidence is that most departments operate in a condition of tension between those who see career training as central and those who would take a more critical, theoretical direction. Inevitably, the entrenched professional approach wins out in most of these conflicts, due to the burden of accomplishing its time-consuming mission and due to the pressure of student desires for job-training (desires fostered by the self-definitions of departments and the celebratory pedagogy of professional teachers).

There is no shortage of faculty in media studies who wholeheartedly endorse the professional approach. Their views are expressed in position papers and essays disseminated through the various professional organizations in the field (particularly, the Broadcast Education Association, the Association for Education in Journalism and Mass Communication and some divisions of the Speech Communication Association). An examination of this discourse of professionalism shows it to be rooted not in a pedagogical theory, nor in a model of social relevance, but rather in instrumental "realities."

This discourse is, first, rooted in a conception of education that models itself on the market. As David Hazinski (1989) argues, "to say that communications education now serves 'the industry' is to forget the most important educational client of all, the communications student." Hazinski goes on to argue that calls for liberal arts curricula in media education are the domain of academics removed from the real world of the marketplace, and that they would squander resources that should be directed toward helping to "improve the quality of journalists, public relations professionals and advertising executives." He concludes that "the final arbiter for what communications is should be those who do it and those who pay for it," namely the industry. If you want to find out what education should be doing ask the PR firms, ask the ad agencies, ask the fathers who shell out tens of thousands for their children's education, ask the legislator who funds the school (for Hazinski, fathers pay, and, I suppose, mothers watch TV). Hazinski employs a discourse that defines students as "products" or "clients," assesses education in terms of "demand and supply of students," defines the educational sphere as "the market," and so on.

Byron Renz (1987) does not even attempt to argue with the ivory tower academics that Hazinski deplores; instead he simply assumes that the goals of broadcast education are purely career-oriented. He calls for an extension of this professional orientation into further areas such as sales and engineering. His solution for greater efficiency is tracking into career-defined sequences, which he calls interdisciplinary. For Renz, the field of media education is interdisciplinary in that it deals with business, technology, production and broadcast journalism. This truncated definition of the interdisciplinary is rooted in Renz's feeling that the advanced technology and complexity of the industry requires more industrial training, which may mean a tradeoff in liberal education. The limited viewpoint here is most notable in Renz's statement that students "enhance their employability in a wider range of broadcasting occupations," thus becoming able to take on "dual roles common particularly in small market stations—the sales manager who doubles as play-by-play sports announcer," for example (34). That the goals of media education should be reduced to the needs of a broadcast market may be striking in its parochialism, but it is a logical conclusion when one defines pedagogy in terms of its occupational outcomes.

Ray Carroll (1987) takes another approach to defending professionalism: "professionalism is liberal education." By this, Carroll means that we need not "compromise" by emphasizing liberal arts and thus taking time away from occupational goals, because the professional approach should itself provide a liberal education. But what does this entail for Carroll? It means that issues of ethical concern, the knack of "getting it right and choosing the right word" and knowledge of the history of the great journalists should be a part of a broadcast journalist's education. In other words, factors of liberal education that add to the training of the journalist determine their place within the overall curriculum.

What is evident in this discourse of professionalism is a pedagogy rooted in a transmission model of education and a complete divorce of pedagogical concerns from cultural politics. While maintaining the need for liberal education, this rhetoric actually empties it of any political import. Again, it is not simply that job training is present as a goal that we question, but rather that the concerns of the market dictate the terms of pedagogical encounter. Under these conditions, the formation of knowledge is not reflected upon, but rather pedagogy is conceived as a practice simply placed on top of an already existing set of conditions (as Hazinski would have it, let the public relations executive define your task, then bring in your pedagogy). We need now to turn more directly to this question of the pedagogical encounter.

Education versus Schooling

The pedagogy of professionalism supports a transmission model of education in several respects. First of all, students are seen as clients in terms of their position of entry into the pedagogical encounter. These clients have defined their objectives in terms of needs through the filter of a vaguely perceived conception of what the broadcast industry wants. Thus, they are willing to enter into the pedagogical encounter on the terms of a predefined set of needs that professionally oriented faculty feed back to them. Although the department conceives of its role as serving these clients at the entry point, the terms of pedagogical encounter shift as the educational process takes place. Now, the students are the employees and the faculty the bosses, standing in for the broadcast industry bosses who have defined the needs of media education.

As employees, students are in a weakened position, one in which they stand as empty vessels to be filled. The professionals have the skills, the knowledge, the techniques and the equipment "know-how," and this is offered to the students as payment. As we noted in chapter 1, this is a model of schooling as opposed to education. As schooling, professional pedagogy is normalizing and controlling. Its impetus is not toward a democratic curriculum, one that encourages active subjects who grapple with the concrete problems of social and personal life.

Professional education also leads toward a transmission model of education in its specific pedagogy. The level of detail in skills acquisition, the rigid breakdown of roles of crew structure, the constant insertion of voices of authority from successful broadcast industry practitioners, and the time-consuming rote learning of formats and managerial models all lead to a form of schooling requiring the student to sit still and listen. Student voice is, indeed, silenced in this process, replaced with the ventriloquist voice of broadcast buzz words.

Other voices in the field have called for a reversal of this professional trend and have drawn on the liberal arts model of education in redefining the task of media education. Thomas Bohn (1988) proposes that professional training can be redefined as not meaning vocational training: "Professionalism does not mean the unquestioned acquisition of unexamined standards and norms; rather, it suggests the ability to reason and analyze complex issues and problems and to place them in appropriate and meaningful contexts" (18). Such an approach takes a direction away from the current professionalization of the field, but we will question whether this accommodation goes far enough. As was noted in chapter 1, the tendency of liberal arts inflections on professional education is to empty out the cultural and political import of critical thinking, defining it more in terms of "thinking skills" and ethical dictates arising from the discipline. Simply placing mass communication in the liberal arts does not solve the problem. When media study is placed in the liberal arts it is discursively underdefined, resulting in its marginalization or in its being placed within liberal pluralist traditions.

The liberal arts cannot in themselves bring about a critical pedagogical approach to media study. First, the traditional notions of isolated disciplines must be questioned. A critical pedagogy of communication is inherently interdisciplinary and would lead to the formation of a cross-disciplinary practice. This points to the fact that there is no easy solution to the problem of the institutionalization of media pedagogy. However, at least Bohn's approach is a first step in the direction of reversing the pedagogy of transmission that is endemic to the vocational training of professionalism.

As we have noted, almost all departments structure their curriculum around career tracks or skill areas. One needs only to look at other disciplines to see the oddity of this approach. In chemistry, for instance, one generally acquires a general chemistry degree, but may track into organic, inorganic, atomic chemistry, polymer science, and so on. These areas have career implications, but are not defined as occupational areas; rather, they are areas within a field of study that requires a theoretical base. In mass communication, tracks are broken down into such areas as broadcast production, broadcast journalism, broadcast management, and so forth. This division directly states that the tracks are for jobs.

The practice of tracking is a discursive practice that defines forms of knowledge as instrumental (in Habermas's terms, technico-rational) and creates a disciplinary situation. This tracking is disciplinary both in compartmentalizing knowledge into units defined as "controlled areas of technique" and in producing a supervisory discipline of control over pedagogic practices and student activities. Tracking further replicates the disciplinary control of the industry through transmitting the practices and codes of the dominant industry discourse.

A further implication of tracking and the transmission model has been the creation of a division between "academic" and "applied" classes of faculty. As we have already noted, the broadcast education field early on relied on faculty drawn from the industry, who in some ways set the tone for the field. The situation today—the proliferation of graduate programs and thus the creation of a pool of Ph.D.s for faculty positions—has changed in some respects, but the division between applied or "special title" faculty and academic or research faculty still persists. This has created a situation of extreme tension. In practice, four different types of faculty can be distinguished: (1) applied faculty, retired from the industry or only active part-time in it, who conceive of academic preparation as non–real world and counterproductive; (2) applied faculty who have gone back to graduate school and who adopt an accommodation approach in terms of the mix of academic and professional study; (3) academic faculty who have had short stints in the industry, but whose primary interests lie in the academic study of a particular area of media, and who also are more accommodating toward a mix of pro and academic study; and (4) academic faculty whose primary interests are in research in mass communication and who view any professional faculty as necessary but second-class.

In research universities these divisions usually result either in a steady-state situation of dominant academic power over an underclass of applied faculty or in all-out warfare between "green eyeshades" (journalists) and "quantoids" (researchers). In the majority of universities and colleges the situation is reversed—applied faculty hold court over departments defined as professional training grounds, while academics attempt to make do. Given the already significant restraints of media education (its overenrollment and intensive pedagogy of careerism), the tensions of faculty divisions create an almost intolerable situation, where thinking about pedagogical issues gives way to logistical squabbles and petty battles over resources.

The False Promise of Jobs

As noted in chapter 1, the idea that the university can be a pathway to employment holds less and less validity. Yet, this is the edifice upon which the professional approach is built. The actual vocational skills learned in broadcast programs are more and more out of date as technology advances more and more quickly. In addition, these skills are usually provided in entry-level training at the employment site anyway. In addition, the employment boom in communication industries has tapered off, as evidenced in the decreased hiring in broadcast markets. Communication industry owners have pushed for efficiency and double duties for employees, thus reducing the need for trained personnel at the production level. As concerns management positions, it is comic to support a view that there are entry-level positions in management. The professional approach's promise of a job is simply a false promise, attractive in attaining high enrollment figures of eager job-seeking undergraduates, but ultimately detrimental to the pedagogical situation.

The futility of a direct "skills for jobs" approach is evidenced in a survey conducted at a large school of communication (AEJMC, 5). The survey showed that graduates were working in over 100 discrete job categories. A further study of all southern schools showed that only 8 percent of graduates had jobs in communication-related fields. Surveys at schools where the authors have worked show that of this 8 percent or so who obtain jobs, only 5 percent remain in the field for over three years. This calls into question the practices of the vocational approach of most departments. Not only are they attracting students via a lie, they are doing so at the cost of pedagogy that could be directed at the real needs of students to continue to develop as active critical citizens involved in choices that determine their futures.

As Robert Blanchard (1988b) states, "We have students, but no status." That is, the communication field continues to garner resentment from the rest of the academic community for its artificially induced popularity and at the same time is falling behind the national trend toward liberal arts education. Kitross (1989) best describes this situation: "There is a mounting fear of an emerging emptiness in our field, a fear that instead of learning ethics, morals, theory, history and logic, students are given one-dimensional teaching of something superficial that can easily be taught in trade school or an operating studio." There is evidence that even the students are more aware of the futility of vocationalism than professional pedagogues. A survey conducted by Porter and Szolka at the University of Missouri-Columbia showed that 63 percent of students preferred to be in a nonprofessionally oriented program.

The Hidden Curriculum of Media Education: Economic Allegiances and the Reproduction of Dominant Practices

The hidden curriculum of media education has been revealed in the previous sections. That which lies underneath the stated goals of training in professional procedures is the practice of inducing compliance to the status quo of the media industry and the corporatist ideology that it supports. The media's construction of a discourse of "cultures as markets" is replicated in the discourse of professionalism. The professional approach depoliticizes the media themselves, turning attention away from the manner in which the media serve as an instrument of dominant ideologies and at the same time foreclosing opportunities to explore the possibilities for resistance to the unification of culture under the sign of the commodity. As a result of the predominant pedagogy of separating theory and practice, the nature of media production and the tools needed to decipher and counteract its hegemony are effectively defeated. Theory is relegated to the wasteland of the ivory tower, forever defined as outside of "real world" knowledge.

Media education pays a price for its allegiance to the industry: its pedagogy is out of its control. But this price is not paid back to media departments; its allegiance to the industry is not reciprocated. The industry, itself, remains smug toward academia, accepting its provision of a source of cheap labor, but disdainful of its theoretical "hogwash." Just like the professional educators within the university, the broadcast industry pays lip service to liberal education, but its actual recommendations to media education always chastise it for not tooling up the right workers. As Robert Blanchard (1986b, 28) puts it,

Like the generals and admirals who are always fighting the last war, the media professionals would have us teach topical, if not yesterday's skills on ephemeral technology in a passing industrial and personnel environment. While steadfastly singing the praises of "the liberal arts," they would limit our priorities to that of entry-level media prep schools designed to meet every passing need from supplying cheap labor to recruiting minorities.

Finally, at the core of this hidden curriculum lies the agenda of the New Right. The professional curriculum supports the goals of the New Right's definition of education—a redirection of resources to the support of industry. Media education becomes one more tool in increasing economic productivity in order to salvage America's hegemony in international capitalism. Certainly, the communication and information industries are primary in the plans of corporatist and governmental structures for the retooling of American economic production in the age of the service economy. In addition, the attention that the professional approach takes away from the cultural and political analysis of the media and its part in the dissemination of capitalist, consumerist values backhandedly supports the New Right's agenda for cultural politics—that is, the return to "American" values. The final outcome is a media pedagogy that supports the New

Right's strategy of disconnecting higher education from the development of civic learning and public commitment to democratic participation.

NOTE

1. The NAB is the major professional association in the television industry; the BEA is a loosely affiliated organization that shares the concerns of that industry. Both organizations hold their annual conventions at the same time of the year in Las Vegas (an apt location for professional organizations that reproduce an endlessly wasteful and hyper-consumptive product). The conventions further serve the purpose of tieing the organizations to the technology industries that produce the equipment of broadcasting (which are on display, complete with bikini-clad "spokesmodels").

Chapter Four

Media Education and the Discourse of the Liberal Arts

INTRODUCTION

Media education in the universities has predominantly emphasized a professional approach that has engendered a separation of theory and practice. In the previous chapter we pitted this professional approach against the idea of liberal arts education, but we must now question whether such a dichotomy is, in fact, fruitful. Has not the liberal arts idea, itself, in a curious fashion, fed into this separation of theory and practice? Although the professional approach, as currently practiced, has in various ways decimated the critical potential of media studies, there may be another way that reintegrates liberal arts and professional modes of education.

We further noted how media education has been displaced in the university, finding no fit within the humanities or social sciences. Neither has it coherently found a place within the institutional structure—it adequately fits into neither schools of arts and sciences nor professional schools. The interdisciplinary nature of media study (is it an art, a social science, a humanity, an industry practice?) points to a displacement that makes it a particularly apt location for discussing the inadequacies of the general definitions of the structure of liberal education.

In order to rethink media education, we must question and rethink the manner in which university education as a whole has been structured through a series of discourses that center around separation, silencing, bifurcation and commodification. We need to address how it is that liberal education functions, what its mission is, its place in the public sphere, the conflicts in current public arguments over its definition and future direction and how the New Right's spin on this has systematically clouded the issues.

WHAT ARE THE LIBERAL ARTS?

Genealogy

How did the idea of liberal education arise? Much of the contemporary debate on this question attempts to trace the idea of liberal education to some kind of originary notion. Further, this genetic origin of the liberal arts is seen as crucial in retrieving its "essence," which then serves as the basis for a call to return to a basic universal definition. Such an approach assumes a smooth history of liberal education and leads to naturalizing the original context of the concept, leading to an erasure of the historical conditions that have at various times connected the idea of liberal education to political, economic and social determinants. Such a fundamentalist approach obscures the contradictory nature of the liberal arts as they have functioned in the last two centuries in the United States.

We choose, instead, to approach the idea of liberal education as an historically situated phenomenon, and will attempt to draw out the discursive framework that has defined it as serving particular political and economic purposes in particular historical conditions. The history of the notion of liberal education is too complex for us to cover in detail. Thus, we will only discuss the general developments that bear upon our project.

The idea of liberal education is often identified with the model of classical education, with its traditional elite status and focus on arts and letters. This ideal has led some to propose that a liberal arts education is concerned with knowledge for its own sake, and should be separated from politics and the social. Such a view has little to do with any actual practice within liberal education's history. As Emil Oestereicher (1991) notes, the liberal arts emerged in the seventeenth and eighteenth centuries in conjunction with the rise of mercantile capitalism and newly forming "democratic" cultures. As such, the liberal arts are partly aimed against the elitist cultural stance of classical education, and thus are practical in the sense of aiming to develop citizenship and participation in the public sphere.

The ideal of liberal education has of course never come about: the golden age of its inception was tainted by the restricted entrance to education, whereby those without property were turned away. Thus, liberal education has always had an exclusionary side to it, based in some notion of educating "the best and brightest" to conduct the business of government and culture. In fact, as Ben-David (1972) points out, prior to 1860, the purpose of liberal university education was to shape the character of the student according to the code of the "gentleman." This was accomplished through discipline—the mind and body of the student were disciplined through study of the classics and attainment of religious piety. Although elitist, such a view tied education to practical political goals.

At some point in the nineteenth century, any connection of liberal education with practical politics was erased and the liberal arts became depoliticized. The idea of a liberal arts education that would engender political practice and critical citizenship (even if a truncated view of being critical) simply could not survive the contradictions between political democracy and capitalist accumulation. Yet, the liberal arts have retained some vestige of this tradition of critical citizenship, and calls for the renewal of the liberal arts are often connected to this tradition.

At the same time that the liberal arts were being depoliticized and emptied of practical value, a practicalization of higher education was occurring in a completely different inflection. The burgeoning capitalist economies, particularly in the United States, required a new vocational training that could correspond to the continual specialization and compartmentalization of labor. Thus, the universities emerged in the later nineteenth century; tied to business and to technological growth, these schools and their benefactors pushed strongly for vocationalism as a primary goal of higher education. This led, in part, to the specialization of academic endeavor and to the generation of departments defined by definite territories and often demarcated by practical and vocational interests (Scott, 1983). It is in the twentieth century that the academic system in the United States has been fully formed through the influential (and politically tied) monetary endowments connected to foundations, corporations and government war efforts (hot and cold).

Thus, as Bowles and Gintis (1976, 202) note, "higher education has been integrated into the wage-labor system." Whereas early educationalists could argue for a nonvocational higher education, today it makes no sense to argue that higher education should be purely classical in its form and content. Instead of a monolithic purpose for higher education, we have a number of functions being served at different levels in a hierarchical structure. Generally, at the highest levels, the elite liberal arts schools, affordable by only the most wealthy, still retain the liberal arts function of training a core of leaders. At a secondary public level, state schools and research universities provide the technicians capable of specialized tasks (although requiring some humanities to "round out their education"); at the lowest levels, the commuter colleges and community colleges provide "skilled" labor. Of course, higher education nowhere simply follows the dictates of capital. There are fundamental contradictions between the mandates of universities and the needs of industry. At all levels of college education, some elements of liberatory education come through. As Bowles and Gintis (1976) state,

It is simply impossible for higher education to conserve its traditional liberal arts structure and to transmit useful high-level skills to students without, at the same time, developing some of the students' critical capacities and transmitting some of the truth about how society operates. (206)

The contemporary university is characterized by discourses and practices that have been worked out since the turn of the century: the contradictory models of liberal and general education, the increasing departmentalization of disciplines, the increasing connection of research with military-industrial purposes, the professionalization of the professorate, the advance of technical knowledge and technology-driven pedagogy, and so on. At the same time that these factors have led the university away from a conception of Dewey's notions of "liberating education," they have created the contradictions that allow the role of criticism and politics to reenter the discursive terrain.

This is evidenced today in the calls by both liberal and conservative politicians and educators for a return to the liberal arts. As we noted in chapter 1, this return to liberal education is matched by a concurrent call to increase the productivity and applicability of American education. Both movements are a reaction to a perceived crisis in higher education. Educators on the left see this crisis as connected to the increasing specialization and technicization of the curriculum. As Barbara Ann Scott (1983) states it,

Criteria of efficiency and expediency now more than ever dictate the content of the curriculum and threaten to suffocate any bona fide intellectual culture. Under the directives from academic policy planners, the new curricular focus is twofold: a reemphasis upon the practical and the mass marketing of the higher learning. . . . The result [is] the gradual erosion of the theoretically oriented liberal arts tradition—the bedrock of higher learning. (215)

For Aronowitz and Giroux (1985) this transformation of higher education is connected to the reduction of the university to providing "social credentials" and functioning as a "mass technical training institute." The liberal arts, far from standing against the practical, far from "producing liberated individuals," have become simply breadth requirements for technocrats and business administration majors. For critical pedagogy, the current problem with higher education is twofold. First, it no longer serves as a guarantee of employment and instead serves as "cultural capital"; this is the problem of "credentialization." Second, it no longer serves to educate individuals to be critical citizens (if it ever did). Under these conditions, the liberal arts have been devalorized. There is no longer any sense of what they are good for.

For the New Right, the problems of higher education are the exact reverse. The crisis in higher education is evidenced in declining academic standards, a flight from teaching toward research, the fragmentation of knowledge, "the corrosive inroads of cultural relativism, and the politicization of the curriculum" (Oakley, 1992, 268). On the surface, the New Right's position points in the same direction as the liberal critiques cited above; however, its actual trajectory is exactly the opposite. This position is motivated by a nostalgia for universal values connected to a patriotic, elitist project. The neoconservative call for fixed canons, discipline, value-neutral methods and teacher authority are rooted in a conception of culture as a given body of information with a fixed meaning. This body of knowledge is to serve as the foundation for the construction of a certain moral character in the individual that serves as the motivational base for "productive life," that is, a life directed toward the goal of reasserting the dominance of the imperialist American market.

Allan Bloom (1987), one of the most vocal of the adherents of the New Right position on higher education, actually called for a return to the classical model of the liberal arts in which their purpose is to provide "a unified view of nature and man's place in it." Henry Giroux (1992) summarizes the politics of this position:

Under the guise of attempting to revitalize the language of morality, these critics and politicians [Bloom, Cheney, Silber, etc.] have, in reality, launched a serious attack on some of the most basic aspects of democratic public life and the social, moral, and political obligations of responsible, critical citizens. What is being valorized in this language is, in part, a view of higher education based on a celebration of cultural uniformity and a rigid view of authority; in addition, the new conservative agenda for higher education includes a call to remake higher education an academic beachhead for defending and limiting the curriculum to a narrowly defined patriarchal, Eurocentric version of the Western tradition and a return to the old transmission model of teaching. (92–93)

For Bloom and the New Right, higher education is about training good citizens through the naturalization of classical ideas. This cooptation of democracy then serves as the liberal arts side of the educational equation, the other side being the reinstitutionalization of vocational training as a national patriotic task.

The current crisis in higher education—budget cuts, student aid cuts, calls for a return to teaching, questioning of political motivations, calls for a return to basics—all arose in conjunction with the conservative climate of the Reagan/Bush years. It seems that the ultimate goal of the New Right strategists is to rethink and perhaps even reinvent higher education on the model of the market. The Bush administration called for a redistribution of funds in secondary education—taking funds from the public sector and transferring them to the private sector. In addition, experiments are being conducted in business-run public education. In higher education a private sector already exists and as "education" governors such as Ohio's George Voinovich decimate the public universities, it seems that the conservatives are carrying forth a plan to cut down significantly public higher education.

The ideological discourse that accompanies these material plans is built on a model that reinstitutes the educational goals of the wealthy and powerful by maintaining a division between providing for the cultural education of an elite corps of leaders, while training the masses in industrial tasks. For the New Right the return to the liberal arts must serve the purpose of retrieving the "cultural heritage." Along with this reinstitution of the traditional curriculum, the sciences, math and technical fields must be reinvigorated with industrial funding, serving the purpose of returning America to its "number one" status.

But as Aronowitz and Giroux (1985) have pointed out, the seeds of a more radical interpretation are contained in the liberal tradition:

The liberal arts are not only the foundation of the bourgeois claim to be the inheritor of western culture; they are also the condition for acquiring critical thinking in a society where the old labor, socialist and radical public institutions that provided these amenities have all but disappeared. That is, in the wake of the nearly complete transformation of the cultural balance of social power towards the technocratic classes, a new terrain of cultural struggle is within the universities, especially the battle for the traditional critical curriculum. (173)

We can see this potential played out even in as traditional a statement as that of James Carey on the liberal tradition in journalism education: "It emphasizes the general, ethical point of view, the oral tradition, the ideals of public life, the process of slow discussion, debate, evidence and argument on which rationality is founded" (Carey, 1978, 847). Such a statement can be interpreted as supporting the status quo position of a Bloom or Silber, but on the other hand, the generality, value orientation and critical thinking component of liberal education slides rhetorically into a more radical sphere of discourse.

In a discourse of critical pedagogy, the components of critical thinking that make up the liberal arts are motivated by a basic drive to "actualize the human abilities to question, to think even about thinking itself, to see things from many different perspectives, to move between languages" (Minnich, 1992, 196). Such a form of critical thinking is political and cultural as opposed to the classical liberal definition, which sees critical thinking in terms of simply "thinking skills." Reading this politics into Carey's statement is exactly the kind of discursive move that infuriates the New Right; they vehemently oppose the politicization of the liberal arts. Bloom, Silber, Dinesh D'Souza, Lynn Cheney, William Bennett and Charles Sykes all whine incessantly about the infusion of politics into the curriculum of contemporary higher education. The problem, however, is not that education has become more political, but that its politics has been exposed because of the current conflicts and differences occurring in our culture. There has never been a nonpolitical universal culture or educational curriculum. As Barbara Herrnstein Smith states, "Politics or ideology is always part of education, but an invisible part so long as everyone agrees—or appears to" (1992, 10). This is exactly what Allan Bloom wanted—an invisible politics, and one in which everyone agreed with him.

This is, in fact, the story of the liberal arts that we have uncovered—a story of constant political and cultural struggle, a story of contradictions and dead ends, a story of material pursuit and the struggle for power and empowerment. In order to get further under this notion of the liberal arts, we need to pinpoint the discursive framework that now operates to define it in such a way that casts doubt on its potential for a cultural politics and a critical pedagogy.

Archeology of the Liberal Arts?

We have looked at a number of debates over what the liberal arts are: they may be defined in terms of function, mission, values, goals, curriculum, forms of thinking, and so forth. But none of these defining strategies really fully gets at what the liberal arts are as they exist in practice or what they might be in some future practice. We do not desire to add to the definitions, but rather to analyze the discourse of liberal education in its current complexity in order to uncover the silent operation of fragmenting and separating practices that we believe problematize the whole project of the liberal arts.

We want to pit the actuality of the liberal arts in their institutional setting against the kind of grand vision of liberal education proposed by John Dewey and others. Dewey saw the purpose of a liberal education as providing the opportunity for people to involve themselves in the deepest problems of society, to acquire the knowledge, skills and ethical responsibility necessary for "reasoned participation in democratically organized publics" (quoted in Giroux, 1992, 96). Such an idealized vision of liberal. education comes straight up against the actualities of power as practiced in university institutions. Particularly, the fragmentation of studies and research discourages students and teachers from dealing with a "whole" problem. This compartmentalization and standardization of research and teaching make it virtually impossible to consider the larger social consequences of intellectual work (Bowles and Gintis, 1976). These and other practices have systematically structured liberal education away from the kind of moral, political vision of Dewey.

In order to bust open this depoliticization of liberal education, we will conduct an archeology of its discourse (loosely modeled on the method of Foucault). In doing so we do not intend to see liberal education as some kind of unity, or as progressively maturing; nor do we attempt to find its internal logic, its origin, or its deep structure. Rather, we hope to locate the discursive practices that have delimited the field of liberal education's actions, fixed its norms for operation and determined its exclusions and choices. In other words, we want to find out why this particular practiced discourse presents itself as applicable to only a certain number of uses and why it limits itself to certain positions and sites. In questioning this discourse of liberal education we find three primary areas of practice: (1) the separation of work and leisure, (2) the preservation of a culture that nowhere exists and (3) the separation of use value and exchange value in the commodification of knowledge.

The Separation of Work and Leisure

The discourse on education is loaded with concepts, terms and values borrowed from the language of the market. This discourse, put into practice, has had profound effects on both learning and teaching. The liberal arts have been articulated in relation to the nature of work and the production of culture through the adoption of a separating, silencing discourse. As Elizabeth Kamarck Minnich (1992) puts it, the "liberal arts" were defined in juxtaposition to the "servile arts." The liberal arts were for free men, those who did not have to work, those who ruled and thought. The development of the idea of liberal education retains some of this dichotomizing in continually relating the function of the liberal arts to the sphere of work, but in such a way that work, leisure and culture are articulated as separate spheres in an economy of political, social life.

The practical outcomes of such a bifurcation are humorously portrayed by Gerald Graff:

English departments characteristically tell students that if they major in English they will learn to become independent thinkers who will fearlessly question the established beliefs and institutions of their society but that, additionally, they will acquire the skills that will qualify them for the professions. If you study English, you will learn how to see through corporate capitalism while qualifying for a job at IBM! (1988, 13)

Thus, the student is asked to be critical in one life, productive in another. The liberating function of the "liberal arts" is practiced in leisure, yet it can be detached from this critical practice and applied in the sphere of work.

For teachers and administrators the liberal arts are discursively practiced as "work that is not real work," that is, as if there is a difference between the real world of work outside in the productive industrial and informational sectors, and the ivory tower of academic work, which is supposed to remain detached from instrumentality. Thus, on the one side liberal education describes itself as instrumentally, yet tangentially, related to the real world of work, while on the other side it stringently detaches itself from any relation to the tainted "reality" of work or the market. The result in both cases is that academic work is not taken seriously, either by administrators or by the public, which has very little access to it anyway. What is missing from this delineation of work is any conception of how teaching and research can be articulated together as work that matters (Herron, 1988).

On the one side we have a view of liberal education as simply an end in itself, on the other a view that subsumes liberal education under the instrumentality of the market. The problem is not one of "reality" but rather of how this discourse has separated theory from practice, and culture, leisure and knowledge from work. The problem of reuniting culture and work is confounding, because it is rooted, in the first place, in a fragmenting discourse. On the one side, the scholar in the academy does not want to reduce the function of research and teaching to the production of a work-force, but on the other side, how can she justify those practices as a kind of work worth carrying out? In the dominating terms of the market there is little else that one can do, except make arguments for the liberal arts as skills training for developing the types of actions and thought that will "work" in the higher levels of employment. There is certainly some truth to this, but the circular position of academic public relations, mentioned by Graff above, points to the manner in which the discourse of the market traps it in a logic that depoliticizes and ultimately castrates liberal education.

A further problem is that for politicians, policy makers and the general public, "real" cultural work (i.e., the work that matters) is not done in the academy, but rather by artists, media workers and creative journalists. One song by the rap group Public Enemy carries more cultural weight than a thousand articles on the deconstruction of texts. It is odd that popular music does this "work" purely in the realm of leisure, whereas the academy's output seems to have a place neither in the real world of work nor in leisure. Of course, for the elite tradition, such popular culture work is precisely "work," because it both makes money and aims for a purpose beyond disinterested contemplation. In this thinking, true cultural work is done for its own sake.

Ira Shor and Paulo Freire have attempted to overcome this problem by reinterpreting the relationship of education to work. Such a reinterpretation requires connecting the classroom to the outside world, while at the same time realizing that they are not the same. For Shor and Freire, traditional education mystifies the world of work, that is, it is silent about the political and ideological dimensions of the market. Shor and Freire state:

The traditional educator and the democratic educator both have to be competent in their ability to educate students around skills needed for jobs. But the traditionalist does it with an ideology concerned with the preservation of the establishment. The liberating educator will try to be efficient in training, in forming the educatees scientifically and technically, but he or she will try to *unveil* the ideology enveloped in the very expectations of the students. (1987, 68)

Although commendable, their view is still trapped in the contradiction between work and the critical. Shor and Freire recognize this contradiction, but relying on modernist concepts of ideological critique and the consciousness of the subject, they are unable to see how the practices of science and "training" are themselves formative of affective subject identities that fragment consciousness and separate practices into nonintersecting domains. Shor and Freire note this very problem: "There is now a radical separation in the curriculum between the programs that do the most concrete training for jobs [engineering, accounting, etc.] and the programs that do the most critical reflection [history, philosophy, etc.]" (70).

Ultimately, Shor and Freire are unable to offer any concrete program that undercuts the loss of relevance of the liberal arts in the face of the vocationalization of training. The primary reason for this failure is that they are unable to extricate themselves from the dichotomy of work versus culture. As Jerry Herron notes,

The problems confronting the academy result from a disconnecting of inside and outside—culture and work, art and life—with the result that nothing real can go on here, least of all, work. Therefore, what has to be done is a reintroduction of inside to outside, "us" to "them." (1988, 133)

One can extend this critique to the interconnected distancing dichotomies that arise from the discourse of modernist political and cultural practice—theory/practice, public/private, labor/leisure, teaching/research, knowledge/morals. All of these, in part, stem from the validation of a contract to labor in commercial terms, and the resulting economization of private and public life. Such a view is akin to the vulgar Marxist theorization of a primary base and a secondary superstructure, relegating the cultural to secondary status. Yet, even in Marx, the misrepresented source of this dichotomy, we can see the lineage of a critique of the bifurcation of manual and intellectual labor, and of the artificial separation of a sphere of work and leisure. Marx idealized a form of society not in which work would stand apart as something alien to a laborer, but rather in which production of all kinds (manual, intellectual, cultural, industrial, etc.) would be seen as united in that they are forms of human activity—thought realized in action.

In this view, culture is the "practico-inert," the lived experience of individuals that is constructed and reproduced in institutions, practices and habits. Cultural forms are not set apart in a realm of abstractions, but rather function in "sustaining a society's division of labor and social hierarchy" (Aronowitz, 1981, 80). The isolation of culture from the "real world" of labor and politics hides the workings of cultural discourses and forms in support of a hierarchy of labor and a fragmentation of communities. Aronowitz criticizes the program of Marcuse on this basis. Marcuse's solution was to propose that "beyond the sphere of production lay the emancipatory affirmative culture where we would have world enough and time to cultivate our aesthetic talents. Work as leisure would become satisfying because it was not tied to the domination of nature and would be entirely voluntary in this sphere" (Aronowitz, 1981, 107). Such a view not only ignores the political and ideological formation of culture, it again relegates cultural and intellectual practice to the margin. Aronowitz instead insists that any cultural politics wishing to work toward the transformation of present society will have to "develop at the conjuncture of work and interaction, on the basis of a new opposition that wishes to create a new culture, including a new work culture which posits as a goal the abolition of the division between intellectual and manual labor" (108).

Overcoming the work versus culture discourse opens up one possibility for the liberal arts to cure its schizophrenia. By connecting its goals to the directed confrontation of culture/work, liberal education could reinsert itself into the "real world" of the public and private spheres, by conceiving of its utility to the concrete needs of student's careers, not in the sense of job training in the presently defined market, but rather, as Barbara Ann Scott (1991, 42) says, in "exposing the context of values and institutions which determine what kind of work is going to be available and what it will be like."

Preserving a Culture That Doesn't Exist

We have seen that the central contradictions of liberal education's use-value are part and parcel of its situation in the wider social conjuncture. Not only does its relation to the world of work need to be reconceived, but its notion of culture has deflected its purposes from anything resembling a critical pedagogy. Part of this is simply a matter of the historical evolution of the university. The notion of college education as the learning of the discipline of culture simply does not make sense in the contemporary conditions of the democratization of higher education, its corresponding connection to the training of a technical workforce, and its function in credentializing students for employment. In concrete practice, the possibility of returning to an elite model of the university (in our argument, undesirable anyway) is impossible. The university is inextricably bound to have both a vocational and a general education component. The question is how these will either be separated or integrated.

The discourse of the New Right holds for a form of integration (in terms of purpose) that is actually an absolute separation (in terms of a theory of what "work" is). Dinesh D'Souza, Lynn Cheney, Roger Kimball and others have called for a return to a traditional model of culture. In this view, as we have mentioned throughout, education has a twofold purpose. First, on the cultural side, it should preserve and reproduce the best values and knowledge of the great works of Western culture and the American way of life. The cultural becomes a depository of essential knowledge and timeless truths, the purpose of which is to substantiate the cultural heritage. Thus, liberal arts become a means of homogenization and a bulwark against the differences generated in a multicultural society. Second, on the vocational side, scientific training and technological advancement, particularly in information services, are conceived as the means for regimenting the workforce and increasing the efficiency of production to insure America's position in the world economy.

Here is the traditional separation of culture and work, but drawn together in a common project—the depoliticization of education, the maintenance of the capitalist system and the disciplining of the social body in order to insure the continuance of the status quo. What is most remarkable in the call back to culture is that the essentialized body of truths that are supposed to define it simply do not exist.

The theoretical and empirical work of pragmatism, the Frankfurt School of critical theory, Kuhnian philosophy of science, structuralism, poststructuralism and feminism have all undermined the notion that any absolute truth exists. This body of research presents overwhelming evidence against any notion that a common American culture exists and that such a culture is grounded in essential and natural truths about humanity. The recent debates over multiculturalism and cultural diversity point to an actually existing conflict of political, ideological and cultural identities, but, in a sense, these are not new findings—a moral, ethnic, class and gendered diversity has always existed in American culture. Feminism has been in the forefront in pointing out the errors of the traditional approach to culture, showing that the male-dominated culture of the Western tradition is exclusionary and based on logical and empirical misrepresentations. As Minnich (1990) points out, the dominant tradition relies on: (1) a faulty generalization in which a hierarchically invidious monism erases difference and ends in taking the few to represent all; (2) circular reasoning based on faulty standards and false claims to neutrality that result in excluding the cultures of diverse class, ethnic and gendered groups; (3) mystified concepts that are either worn smoothly into platitudes or "fraught with emotion and/or taboo and confusion." As Minnich states,

It is assumed that the liberal arts liberate, that they counter human limitations, enrich human abilities. But can they do so while we retain the old monistic hierarchy, which, despite the pairing of terms, does not create mind and body, knowledge and action, theory and practice even as separate but equal? Certainly not so long as those paired terms continue to reflect the same errors we have been exploring, errors in which all that has to do with the "lower" human activities is defined as appropriate to women and lower-caste men, and so as improper for the educated "free man" (1990, 118.)

The New Right's discourse on the liberal arts remains tied to a model of culture as a set of homogeneous values and beliefs that can be imposed only by undemocratic means. Further, this culture, the culture of literary canons, is no longer the culture that matters, that makes up the background of successful citizens. The culture of the Ross Perots, the Bill Clintons and the Donald Trumps is not the humanistic culture of Matthew Arnold and Allan Bloom, it is the culture of movies, television, sports and the popular press (Graff, 1988). This is the culture that connects with the world of work and makes a difference in the lives of those grappling with issues in everyday life. By relegating culture to the nostalgic realm of literary canons, the liberal arts tradition removes itself from the contradictory and diverse culture of everyday life that matters in democratic life. This is simply to say that our conception of culture must be a more inclusive one, along the lines of Raymond Williams's definition of it as "a whole way of life." The cultural studies argument is simply that culture must be seen as inclusive of diverse and dispersed forms of activity that include forms of laboring, styles of individual investment, experiences of textual production and consumption, and all other actions of everyday life.

The disciplinary boundaries of the liberal arts have fettered culture, relegating it to a sphere of status knowledge. This traditional view of culture has led to a monolithic canonization of scientific reason, a naturalization of aesthetic standards of beauty and a validating of the educational system as a cultural medium of acceptance and passivity. A critical pedagogy would attempt to rethink these relationships, seeing culture as a terrain of action grounded in diverse historical struggles. As Peter McLaren (1992, 33) states, "A liberating praxis is not the creation of reason alone, but is based on a reasoning process undertaken as action in and on the world."

The Commodity Fetish of the Liberal Arts

The discourse of the liberal arts takes up its place within the wider discursive terrain of the market, of economy. In the language of politicians, "better schools mean better jobs"; and for students, college means getting a job or a higher income. College education becomes a measurable commodity—the benefit of college measured as its cost versus future salary potential. Public policy is dictated by cost-benefit analysis, thus justifying only those knowledge forms that contribute to economic growth. Curriculum design is dictated by consumer demand and industrial need (Scott, 1991). In such a discourse, marketability, productivity and investment become the key terms; and these terms are applied not just in the technology-driven world of professional education, but in the liberal arts themselves. Marx saw the implications of this ideology in calling the university a "knowledge factory," and Veblen foresaw the effects of the further economization and standardization of university education, stating that

Learning is a marketable commodity, to be produced on a piece-rate plan, bought and sold by standard units; measured, counted and reduced to staple equivalents by impersonal, mechanical tests . . . [which] acts to deter both students and teachers from a free pursuit of knowledge, as contrasted with the pursuit of academic credits. (cited in Scott, 1983, 235)

This vocationalization of the curriculum is supported by the educational "consumer"—the student. But as Scott notes,

Students are assumed to be making voluntary choices that, in the aggregate, create the demand for particular educational commodities or services. Yet this notion of the supposedly sovereign student—determining, in effect, curricular content and instructional styles—is just as fallacious as its counterpart, the sovereign consumer of orthodox economics. Neither takes into account the manipulation of student/consumer taste and the coercion lurking behind the student's/consumer's exercise of choice. (1983, 238)

In media education, the acquiescence to the needs of the student is particularly acute. As mentioned in chapter 3, it is the industry and its presentation of what media study should be and what working in the media is that partially constructs the students' conception of what they need. We then build our programs based on this need, which is not necessarily what students need or want, but rather what the industry has told them they need or should want in order to work in the field.

This commodification of education is most evident in fields that define themselves as applied, but, further, "application" has become an essential self-defining term for all disciplines, including the liberal arts. Philosophy has turned more and more to defining itself in terms of its applicability to furthering science, particularly cognitive science, and at a more mundane level promotes itself as preparation for law school. English promotes itself in terms of developing writing and thinking skills necessary for upper-level management jobs.

The problem with such a notion of applicability is not that use-value is a tainting of "the tradition" or in itself an invalid goal. Rather it is that use-value is defined and negated by exchange-value. As Giroux notes,

They [teachers] become focused on a fetishized methodology that precludes examination of their roles as public intellectuals, of the institutions in which they work, and of society at large. The language they learn or take up is depoliticized; it is largely a language of procedure and technique. (1992, 155)

In this manner, the liberal arts take up all those contemporary practices that erase the first order utility of education—its formation, revaluation and critique of knowledge in the service of opening up the possibilities for students to become active public individuals involved in decision-making processes that affect the political, economic and cultural life of a radical democracy. These separating and silencing practices include: the commodification of knowledge, the construction of the student as consumer, the practice of competition as the defining mode of activity (through entrance exams, the grading system, etc.), the creation of hierarchies of all types—

among schools, departments, faculty and students—and the adoption of the technology of information as the sine qua non of knowledge and success.

Knowledge itself becomes the ultimate commodity. Liberal education becomes a machine for the production of the degree commodity defined in terms of its value for career advancement. This value is not calculated in terms of knowledge acquired, but rather through an abstract calculation of exchange-value based in credentialization, ranking of the educational institution and department, and a fetishization of the degree as the marker of a knowledge that promises the smooth transfer to applicability in the market.

The discourse of the liberal arts centered around a separation of work and culture, a centrist misrepresentation of culture as homogeneous and given, and a commodification of education has produced a condition of schizophrenia for the university. Able neither to fulfill its role in reproducing the culture or its role in providing skills for its "clients" to acquire jobs, liberal education has lost a cogent sense of its purpose. This is the context for looking at media education in the contemporary university; we now return to look specifically at media education and its place in the liberal arts and professional education.

MEDIA EDUCATION AND THE LIBERAL ARTS

Return to Schizophrenia

Media education is in a sense a boundary discipline; in fact, not a discipline at all, situated between the purely industrial purposes of the professional school and the contradictory stances of the liberal arts. It, more than the traditional humanities, rehearses the discourse of separation, silencing and commodification in an exemplary manner, and in doing so it more directly shows the traces of its schizophrenia on the surface. Yet, media education also holds a certain promise; for in taking up a contradictory, underdefined space in the university it brings forth its contradictions openly: the separating practices are on the surface of its practice, not hidden in traditions and formative bifurcations engendered by the systematic discursive entanglements of the history of the idea of the liberal arts. This being said, we must locate media education within the overall discourse that has defined the university and has localized, at least in part, media education's self-reflection within the same discourse of liberal education that we addressed above.

Media Education's Underdefinition and Confusion of Purpose

Whereas the traditional liberal arts have suffered from a form of overdiscursification, media education has suffered from underdefinition and a lack of direction. But this has resulted in a similar confusion of purpose to that suffered by the disciplines in the liberal arts. The schizophrenia inherent in the self-defining of liberal arts through the separation of work and culture is played out in a hyper-separation in media education. Media education not only takes up a position as a separated and fragmented field in contradistinction to other humanities and social sciences, it is internally specialized and fragmented in a way that is organizationally and practically different than liberal arts fields.

Gerald Graff has located much of the problem of the contemporary humanities in the phenomenon of specialization and fragmentation. But as Graff states,

It is not specialization itself that occasions problems so much as the failure to bring specializations into relation with one another in any planned way. Specialization becomes self-enclosure only when there is no institutionalized correlation of specialities—which means not only no integration but not even any conflict of specialities. It is not ability to *agree* that is intellectually stultifying, as many analysts argue, but inability to *disagree*, for a dispersed set of independent fields can't even add up to an instructive set of antagonisms. (1985, 65)

Graff is saying that the humanities departments of various specialities function to keep faculty separate and out of conflict. In other words, the university functions in a complex way to insure that no one talks to anyone else, and it does so both within the humanities and between the "culture" of humanities and the "work" of the sciences and social sciences. In this manner, the actual conflictual history of the formation of departments is hidden and schizophrenia and alienation become the defining condition of identity in the university.

Media education takes part in this fragmentation in a peculiar way. On the one hand it began not as a self-defined discipline, but as a loose amalgamation of approaches centered in other specializations in the university—social psychology, political science, linguistics, sociology, and so on. As such, it borrows from a dispersed array of fields, but instead of accepting this nonfoundation in interdisciplinary exploration, it attempted to amalgamate its divisiveness by cementing the field of media education within departments defined as specifically mass communication, telecommunication, and so on. As a result, most contemporary departments in media education are as specialized and fragmented from the rest of the university as are the traditional disciplines.

For media education there is a further problem of definition. Whereas departments such as English, history and philosophy are well accepted as isolated disciplines within the academy, media education has never been able to quite achieve this status. The resulting situation is one where internally it operates as a separate sphere of knowledge and discipline, while externally it continually has to justify its existence to the greater university. Further, internally, media education, although self-defined as a discipline, operates in an extremely fragmentary way—it fails to locate its discipline in an object, method, empirical procedure, set of codes, body of texts or theory. Media education incessantly crosses borders and yet denies that it does so. No wonder that it remains confused as to its purpose.

Tacking on Democracy to an Industrial Approach

The two major attempts to provide a disciplinary coherence to the field loosely follow the separating of work and culture that we have discussed. On the one side, some divisions in the field opt for the professional approach, squarely positioning the purpose of education as training for work. On the other side, some departments define their purpose as the social scientific investigation of media as a cultural, psychological phenomena (such departments usually also provide some kind of work-related course work). Various calls to reinsert the liberal arts into the media education curriculum do so in a manner that leaves untouched the separation between work and culture. For example, Blanchard (1988a) addresses approaches to liberalizing journalism education in terms of "placing more liberal arts in our courses" and "requiring a certain number of outside liberal arts courses." In this view, liberal arts becomes an approach that can be integrated into the curriculum—certain courses will have liberal arts content and approaches, others not. The notion that vocationalism can be balanced with liberal education through distribution creates the situation endemic to media education: students line up in droves for professional content courses and resist or merely compliantly sit through courses designated as having liberal arts content.

In splitting the field into its component schizophrenic parts, those responsible for the administrative definition of the field set the conditions for the marginalization of mass communication programs and the resulting bifurcations that still define its approaches to education. In the present state of the field, the liberalization of the media education curriculum forces an even more stringent separation of critical, liberal education functions and professional applications to work, as well as a deepening commodification of the media education "product." What is missing is a discourse of preserving the culture, for unlike the traditional liberal arts, media education never had any authority or tradition of maintaining a cultural project. Instead, its preservation is of a social science project of dubious value, one that defines media education's place in the preservation of American values as a scientific task of preserving, but at the same time reworking, the place of the media industry and state policy in cultural reproduction through the "free market-place of ideas."

Yet, as we have noted in chapter 2, there are certainly countertraditions in the field, for instance that of the Chicago School, which attempted to see media education as connected to the project of democracy. As politically traditional and overly celebratory of the role of communication as these "progressive" views were, they did engender a continuance of concern of the place of media and communication in the furtherance of political community and democracy. However, the current situation is one in which these cultural and political concerns with democracy are simply tacked on to an industrial approach.

In the history of media education, fundamental mistakes were made in dividing and compartmentalizing the field, dividing programs up and placing media education in both journalism programs and speech communication programs. This functioned to split up the study of communication. As the Oregon report, generally regarded as the standard statement on reforming Journalism and Mass Communication education, states,

We educators failed to assume leadership for broad-based communication studies and in the process failed higher education and American society by refusing to be a major force for learning and advancement of knowledge about mass communication in a manner useful for all citizens. Consumer education took a back seat, while professional education was proclaimed premier. (Dennis, 1984)

Despite the misplaced definition of education for citizenship as "consumer education," this statement is to the point. The establishment of dispersed and isolated disciplines over against the inherent interdisciplinary approach of the study of communication as a fundamental social, political and cultural sphere has led to the current situation, which makes rethinking the field in terms of a critical pedagogy an immensely difficult task.

Graff's articulation of how potentially radical approaches are appropriated in the university captures the essence of the present situation in media education. If we substitute "critical media study" for "literary theory" and "media education" for "literature," Graff precisely describes the current impasse:

If institutional history continues to run to form, we can expect [critical media study] to be defused not by being repressed but by being accepted and relegated to the margin where it will cease to be a bother. This indeed has already happened. Instead of being used to create a context of general ideas that might bring the different viewpoints and methods of the [media education] department into fruitful debate, [critical media study] becomes yet another field, a fact which encourages it to be just the sort of self-promoting and exclusionary activity that its enemies denounce it for being. . . . Once [critical media study] has been thus "covered" in the department's table of "areas," the rest of the faculty is free to ignore the issues theorists raise. (1985, 67)

The Politics of Method and Technology

Having missed an opportunity to position itself in the liberal arts, media education is now attempting to incorporate a liberal arts approach into its curriculum. The dominant condition of most departments is the professional vocational approach, discussed in chapter 3; thus, media education for the most part reverses the schizophrenia of the liberal arts, while remaining squarely within its dichotomies. Whereas the problem for the liberal arts is connected to holding on to a neutral aesthetic of culture, thus creating a condition where it has difficulty connecting itself to the sphere of work, media education begins with a wholly industrial discourse on work, finding itself unable to attend to culture.

Attempts to bridge this gap call for the injection of liberal arts methods into the media education curriculum. After-the-fact attempts are made to show how media education courses are liberal in their content anyway. This rhetoric is actually centered in an almost total commodification of education. Professional and liberal arts methods and contents are commodities that each serve a function in attracting students, forming their labor efficiency and selling them to the market. Liberal arts are good for the industry, because they provide additional methods that fit the job market. In some departments the call for breadth in education is simply the recognition that industry would like its workers to have some writing ability, accounting and business courses, and, for news media, some knowledge of practical politics and history.

There is an impetus to move beyond this kind of commodification of knowledge toward a view of media education as media studies. In this view, media education would be more like a literature department in which the media are studied in their own right as an object of understanding and interpretation. This is, in fact, the direction of most graduate programs, where social science and other theoretical methods are applied to the study of the media as a political, social, economic and cultural practice. However, even at the graduate level, most master's programs divide themselves between a project M.A. directed at postundergraduate professional training and a thesis M.A. directed at preparation for doctorate programs. In fact, at most graduate schools, graduate assistants are introduced to the academic condition of schizophrenia where their course work focuses on the critical or empirical investigation of media, while their teaching assistant work is directed at training undergraduates in various professional methods and technologies.

Indeed, the technology of the media is a major impasse for a liberal arts–based media curriculum. Media production courses usually have some statement in regard to the need of students to take a critical approach to the construction of meaning, adding that, of course, the technology of doing video will also be emphasized. A technicist view of the implements of media production neutralizes the potential for any liberal arts content or method in the standard media courses. The curriculum becomes defined in terms of technological tools, as if the political and economic dimensions of media are matters separate from the methods and technologies of industrial programming. As a result, contents, methods, styles of discourse, pedagogical approaches and theoretical components of media education are compartmentalized and separated into isolated domains, finding their possibility for integration only in the instrumentalist workings of the commodity market.

THE CRISIS IN MEDIA EDUCATION

Selling Out Democracy

The schizo-world of media education has submerged any notion of a democratic curriculum in which learning is connected to both the larger world of work and the media's place in cultural politics. The connection to any notion of learning the practice of citizenship as "working" within a transformative democracy has been lost. The crisis of media education is precisely its loss of relevance to the actual life situations of the majority in the United States, to any notion of public philosophy and critical citizenship. Instead, media education, by narrowing itself to the raw world of industrial work, has marginalized itself within the university. It cannot claim to be revitalizing the cultural, either through a critical move or through a naturalization of conservative values. Neither can it claim the validation of the sciences or engineering as theoretical and methodological preparation for high technology professions. Instead, it remains on the margins of validity in the university as a low-level professional field—misunderstood and maligned by both the liberal arts and sciences.

In the long run, it is not of crucial critical importance that media education receive the validation of the university, especially by achieving the same kind of self-serving validation of business schools or the misplaced validation of "high cultural" status of literature departments. Instead, media education must seek to substantiate itself within its own terms, drawing upon the potential it has for developing as an interdisciplinary field of investigation into the technical, political, economic and cultural ramifications inherent in the media—the most powerful force of cultural reproduction in contemporary society.

Ideally, the university as a whole should strive toward the goals of what Giroux calls a democratic curriculum. Such a curriculum would once and for all ditch the abstract separation of knowledge into isolated disciplines such as history, English, and so on, and instead would encourage an active dialogue between fields of knowledge in the university, centered around incorporating themes and issues that address the concrete conditions and problems of adult life. To reiterate Giroux's formulation, knowledge in terms of democratic learning

should include not only the basic skills students will need to work and live in the wider society, but also knowledge about the social forms through which human beings live, become conscious, and sustain themselves, particularly with respect to the social and political demands of democratic citizenship. This relates to knowledge about power and how it works, as well as to analyses of those practices such as racism, sexism, and class exploitation that structure and mediate the encounters of everyday life. (Giroux, 1988, 103)

Such a curriculum is not a call to eliminate tradition, basic skills and practical knowledge in favor of a theoretically radical curriculum divorced from the concerns of students with their futures. Instead, it promises to integrate learning by opening up the silences about the conditions of life in the real world, while at the same time providing opportunities to explore the practical outcomes of theory, method, technique and criticism in transforming that world so as to provide the space for people to further their chances for meaningful employment.

Administrators and Critical Pedagogy

Realistically, the chances for developing a critical pedagogy in media education and in the university in general are limited by the current conditions of economic and political power. A crucial dimension here is the position of administration within the university, which is ruled by a managerial style that precludes the possibility of seeing decision making within the university as anything but instrumental. As Aronowitz and Giroux state.

The recruitment of administrators from faculty ranks is rapidly receding in importance as the academic system has increasingly adopted the corporate managerial practice of recruiting professional managers for high university positions. In many cases, even when administrators hold formal academic credentials these serve as legitimating fig leaves for a professionalized management. (1985, 183)

Administrators in the university have turned away from the concerns of faculty and students toward the manipulation of budgets, the fostering of industry connections, the implementation of criteria of efficiency and the control of the curriculum as a marketable commodity.

This style of management extends downward into the management of departments. For media education this means that professional training and industry ties are often dictated at levels outside of the control of the faculty. The authors have experienced this apparatus of control and discipline in several departments. Faculty become the object of a panoptic power in which their actions are scrutinized to such an extent that to "get along" they incorporate the functioning of this surveillance, becoming the principle of their own subjection.

Overcoming these conditions will require that faculty organize themselves into mutual support groups that work through protest and public debate to reverse the reduction of the university to an arm of industry and the conservative political constituencies that would remake the university on the model of the factory. There are no easy solutions here. The critical pedagogical movement must extend itself into the upper reaches of the university, developing an intellectually effective analysis of "critical administration." Perhaps, the continued efforts of critical pedagogy will produce the possibility where one day we will have pockets of "critical administrators," just as today individual faculty take up the critical pedagogical project in their courses and departments.

Possibilities and Hopes

We need a whole new way of thinking about the university. Media educators cannot expect to transform their situation within an institution defined by the current discourses and practices. Given that we cannot expect a wholesale transformation of the university overnight, we can begin to make the transformation by reconceiving our own practices and working toward the kind of institutional reconceptualization called for by a critical pedagogy. The first step toward this dream is to deconstruct the present answers to the question, "What is a university?" We have attempted to carry out such a critique, but it is time to propose a direction, an alternative to the schizophrenic condition that we inhabit.

Redefining Work

It is crucial to overcome the separation of work and culture inherent in the traditional definitions of general education. We need to rethink the relation of work, leisure and culture in a way that neither separates the cultural practices of learning and teaching from work by seeing liberal education as simply an end in itself, nor simply grafts education onto the instrumental relations of the market. A thorough reworking of the relationship of work to culture (and in media education, the relationship between professionalism and critical liberal arts) means going beyond a practice of simply relating or uniting these two separate domains. We must eradicate the dichotomizing thinking that founds this separating act. This means not reuniting these spheres, but rather, creating through practice a discourse that totally deconstructs this bifurcation.

The silencing and distancing discourses of Western thinking work to create the doubles that condemn media education to the constant struggle between vocationalism and liberal arts: theory versus practice, critical reflection versus training for jobs, skills versus knowledge, art versus life, culture versus work, research versus teaching, and so on. Any attempt to substantiate media education as a discipline by validating the inherent superiority of the liberal arts approach as a pure realm abstracted from the dirty work of the media laborer simply results in marginalizing cultural and intellectual practice. Instead, we must redefine the very action of labor, pulling it out of its domicile in the contradictory realm of the market.

Within the terms of present discourse, work and labor are formulated and identified as labor power. The entire baggage of the capitalist market is attached to our conceptualization of work: the contract, employer versus employee, hierarchy of job functions, the price of labor, selling and buying of skills, the separation of spheres of production and distribution, the dominance of exchange value, supply and demand, the division of labor, and so forth. Within these terms the worker exists in a split identity—as "object for capital" and as "living creative subject" (Harvey, 1982, 114). In the present conjuncture the laboring subject is free to sell its labor power, but the freedom to carry out the act of labor is severely limited and controlled by relations of production.

We must divest ourselves of this conception (and then, this practice) by reconceptualizing work, not as labor power, but as labor in its activity. Work, then, for the student, should not be seen as a separate domain outside and in the future, but rather as an internal dimension of human activity, conceived as a whole. Thus, political practices, cultural practices, self-formation, artistic reverie, play, social interaction and work all coalesce in the development of praxis.

The skill-specific, field-exclusive and job-related focus of media education simply will not do. However, as Aronowitz and Giroux state,

We do not deny that learning skills associated with many occupations can contribute to serious learning. With Dewey we are persuaded that learning can take place *through* occupations, but the point is not to learn a narrow skill which is likely to become obsolete in the near future; we contend that only a multifaceted education can enable students to achieve the autonomy and creativity that a democratic society needs. Learning is a way to power and gratification, but neoconservatives have no program for empowerment, only for providing human capital able to make American business viable once more in the world market. (1985, 215)

Here is the key to reconceptualizing the relation of work and culture in the university and in society at large: work is not something that the market uses, rather it is that which builds a democratic society. There is no better place to start the work of transforming this society into a more radically democratic one, than in media education, given that the media are the most powerful force in setting our cultural agenda. For media education this will mean more than simply adding courses on "media and society." The traditional areas of management, production and planning cannot be left to the professionals, while liberal arts faculty conduct seminars on media criticism. These areas need to be eradicated altogether, that is, as separate courses in "how to labor." Instead, a pedagogy of cultural politics needs to be infused into these territories, redefining them in terms of knowledge useful not only for practicing in the industry, but for furthering the goals of an emancipatory democracy. Such a political project will actually meet the needs of students in their careers by empowering them to integrate their lives of work and leisure through inventing a new culture of work rooted in the goals of a radical democracy.

Stepping Out in Front in Redefining Liberal Education

> This is imagination. This is the possibility to go beyond tomorrow without being naively idealistic. This is Utopianism as a dialectical relationship between denouncing the present and announcing the future. To anticipate tomorrow by dreaming today. The question is as Cabral said, Is the dream a possible one or not? If it is less possible, the question for us is how to make it more possible. (Shor & Freire, 1987, 197)

Critical pedagogy presents a counterattack on the current hegemony of thinking in and about education and a counterproposal for a practice that hopes for a better future. This future dreams of the university as a place: (1) where education develops the abilities of people to become active citizens, working toward a more radical democracy; (2) where difference is recognized as a positive social condition that leads to the discussion of diverse concerns and experiences in the formation of an active and effective public sphere; (3) where theory and practice are integrated in developing practices of critical reflection and concrete action that lead to a creation of a new culture of work; and (4) where educators function as transformative intellectuals who are actively engaged in the concrete concerns of communities and the nation (not disinterested, neutral arbiters of a cultural past).

The present social, political and economic climate makes such a project appear to be an impossible utopian quest. But the point here is not to give in to the pressure to acquiesce to the status quo; with Shor and Freire, we must step out in front in the attempt to dream of an alternative future. This will require hard work, but we must make the first step, by putting forward the dream in such a way that action becomes a possibility. At this point, we can barely imagine how the university might be transformed, but we believe the direction it must take is both evident and morally and politically justified.

First of all, we agree with Scott that "the notion of education must be tied to the vision of a *public sphere*, to the concept of the citizen whose civic duty [is] to practice his wisdom in everyday life" (1991, 16). This goal is prescient today in light of the increasing depoliticization of citizenship and the near disappearance of the public sphere into oblivion. As media educators, we should be in the forefront of reinvigorating education, as our field of inquiry and our sphere of practice are contributory (via the degradation of political life through the media) to this condition. We must step out in front.

How can the university become a public sphere that counters the truncated space of public political discourse established in the media and in our institutions of education that have been won over by the self-serving rhetoric of the New Right? We must develop vital strategies that effectively confront the space of political authority established by the Right. This authority is grounded in a politics that "argues for forms of community life which extend the principles of liberty, equality, justice, and freedom to the widest possible set of institutional and lived relations" (Giroux, 1991, 56). Giroux stresses the importance of reestablishing the importance of the public sphere:

Academics can no longer retreat into their careers, classrooms, or symposiums as if they were the only public spheres available for engaging the power of ideas and the relations of power. Foucault's (1977) notion of the specific intellectual taking up struggles connected to particular issues and contexts must be combined with Gramsci's (1971) notion of the engaged intellectual who connects his or her work to broader social concerns that deeply affect how people live, work and survive. (Giroux, 1991, 57)

Whereas the Right has attempted to define the public sphere in such a way that only issues and values rooted in a "common project of Americanism" can be discussed, the Left's redeployment of the public sphere calls into question what Nancy Fraser (1990, 62) calls its bourgeois masculinist assumptions. According to Fraser, we need to recognize that we cannot bracket the status differentials of individuals as if we were all equals, nor can we assume that a single, unified public sphere is necessarily preferable to a "nexus of multiple publics," and we must question restricting the discourse of the public sphere to the common good instead of "private interests and private issues" (Fraser, 1990, 62). Thus, Fraser calls for the development of various "counterpublics" that

militate against separatism because [they] assume an orientation that is publicist. Insofar as these arenas are publics they are by definition not enclaves—which is not to deny that they are often involuntarily enclaved. After all, to interact discursively as a member of a public—subaltern or otherwise—is to disseminate one's discourse into ever widening arenas. (1990, 67)

This widening of arenas is crucial, both in the sense that various groups have a chance to convince others that their concerns should be added to the agenda of the common good and in the sense of expanding the discursive space of practice to include both public opinion-formation and decision making. The university and the liberal arts should be at the forefront of establishing the ground on which various counterpublics can engage in active dialogue.

If the university is to be transformed in this manner, we need to fashion institutional practices that challenge existing institutions by directly confronting the power relationships through which they govern. This means actively working to create new institutional practices that directly and indirectly impact upon policy decisions. Such a project can only be successful (and avoid the traps of erasing the other and falling back into its own authoritarian structure) by basing itself in a vision of pedagogy and politics such as that laid out by Giroux, one that reworks the concepts of authority and value, and works toward establishing affective commitments to a radical democracy while supporting the interests and struggles of different oppositional groups.

This will require that critical educators work through the issues discussed here in developing new locations of authority and forging a discourse from those locations that connects with people's affective commitments. This means working for and with "the masses" to rediscover those issues and struggles that really matter. In the end, to be effective this practice must be affective, it must work toward reinvigorating public debate through a passionate discourse.

A second task related to the development of the university as a public sphere involves redefining the goals of education in terms of political (in the broad sense) values. In this regard, we agree with Engel:

The renewal of higher education in the Untied States should be based upon two revolutionary values: *democracy* and *social responsibility*. In a democracy people make choices for themselves and others and take responsibility for them. The function of democratic colleges and universities (and indeed, the entire educational system) thus, ought to be teaching people how to make those choices—personal, political, moral, and intellectual. (1991, 191)

And, we add, such a revolutionary project will have to go beyond simply printing flowery words in the college bulletin. In media education, for example, it would mean redesigning our curriculum, rethinking what counts as our core, how we utilize our nonclassroom activities (such as student radio and cable), and how we connect ourselves to industry and other outside agencies. To take such an approach toward education means thinking seriously about what we mean by theory, practice, critical thinking, working and action.

A third task for transforming the university is to rethink what a department is, and resultantly, what a course is. In media education, we have allowed the institutional setting and the standards of what a "true" discipline is to set our agenda. Departments have become bureaucratic machines that, through the implementation of panoptic technologies, predefine the values and goals of education within them as instrumental and managerial. We are, as Graff says, used to being skeptical of the department, "yet we rarely direct the same skepticism at the concept of the course" (1992, 63). Just as departments (and the divisions within them) work to isolate individuals from each other, courses (as singular entities) become isolated from one another. We need to think of courses as existing in a whole that relates them to each other. In media education, with our endless tracking mechanisms and specialized fields, we often work to silence any dialogue between the course work.

Our courses are typically set up to cover an area of operation in the media or a particular object of study, usually connected to another isolated department or discipline (for example, media politics, media and society, media ethics). Such courses then cover their material, which never shows up anywhere else in the curriculum. We need to stop thinking of courses as instrumentalities and instead reconsider the entire structure. Transforming the curriculum is not a matter of adding new ideas about critical thinking to the existing curriculum. Such a practice leads to the addition of a new course to what already exists, resulting in no one having to deal with the new idea's impact on them or what they do. Instead, we need to incorporate the transforming impetus across the entire array of course work. This means not courses on ethics, criticism, social responsibility, politics, critical theory and feminist media studies, but rather ethical, critical, political and feminist theory and practice across the entire curriculum. In addition, we can add Graff's (1992, 57) recommendation here, that "the most educationally effective way to deal with present conflicts over education and culture is to teach the conflicts themselves. And not just teach the conflicts in separate classrooms, but structure them into the curriculum, using them to give the curriculum the coherence that it badly lacks." Thus, the very questions we are raising about media education ought to be a part of media education.[1]

Repositioning Media Education in the University—Liberal Art or Postdiscipline

It is our proposal that media education can move to the forefront in providing an example to the wider university of what a transformed educational practice can be. We make this bold claim based on the present status of media education—it is, as we have attempted to show, entirely muddled and incoherent. Media education exists in a dispersed array of institutional arrangements with widely divergent names; it is unclear as to its past and underdefined in terms of its purpose; it is radically interdisciplinary, although it doesn't know it; it is dimly viewed and low in status; it has no direct connection to elite traditions; it has no coherent method, object of research or theory; it is neither a liberal art nor a social science or it is both. In positive terms, media education is currently in a potentially flexible state, one in which it can, without coming in mortal conflict with an existing tradition, transform itself through beginning anew.

Media education is not a liberal art, neither should it be. This is not to say that it is a professional skill program, or that it is lacking in what a liberal art should be, or that it shouldn't take up a place somewhere in the tradition of liberal education. Rather, it is better to say that media education is the locus for experimenting in the creation of a postdiscipline, a field of action that trashes the old hierarchies and pregiven definitions and instead redefines itself as radically interdisciplinary and democratic. Media education draws upon a number of different disciplines in mapping its object: political science, sociology, history, philosophy, engineering, economics, and so on. Each of these disciplines, as taken up in media studies, tends to be unaware of its representation of the object of study, thus remaining isolated in its own body of theory and method. Within a transformed media studies, the symbolic system's construction of the realities of cultural, political and economic life are pushed to the foreground, for the media itself is the object par excellence for critical analysis of the manner in which knowledge and action are shaped by discursive practice. Thus, media education can draw upon its own refashioning of the tools of various disciplines to assess critically their production of knowledge about the media as constructed and contestable. As a result, the radical interdisciplinarity of media education could become the terrain upon which the very foundations of elite hermetic disciplines are questioned and debated.

It must be clear that we are not proposing that the present condition of media education is moving in this direction, but rather that the cultural studies tradition of media studies, which exists currently as just one more isolated part of it, has the potential to transform media education into this kind of postdiscipline. Of course, the approach we are recommending does have more in common with the liberal arts tradition than with vocationalism, and it may be necessary to retain some political discourse in support of liberal arts, as it still serves as a common catch-all for nonprofessional education. However, we do not want to favor the clean theoretical space of the liberal arts over the dirty world of practical vocation. We need to transform both of them into areas of dirty theory and practice.

We agree with Blanchard and Christ that media education can become an intellectually leading field in the university:

We should be providing media literacy courses to all students. We should be liberating the liberal arts from their tradition-bound specializations. We should be providing the media industry and the public at large with, as Dennis says, "institutional memory," media-society "sense-making," and value-intensive criticism, rather, say, than supplying them free labor, masked as "internships." (1988, 12)

We now need to move directly into the curriculum of media education to uncover its specific problems and potentials. Can we dream today of a media education that hopes for a better tomorrow?

NOTE

1. It should be noted that Graff tends to maintain an elitist position, seeing "the conflicts" as those issues (such as the canon, deconstructive versus traditional criticism, etc.) which high theory has developed within the academy. We adopt Graff's notion to mean instead that pedagogy itself, and particularly as it affects students, should be foregrounded.

Chapter Five

Remaking Media Education

We have seen how media education is currently faced with a number of structural, theoretical and conceptual conditions that mitigate against its developing a critical pedagogy attuned to the goals we believe it should support. First of all, the dichotomy of professionalism versus liberal arts has led to a conception of education as a commodity that is purchased for its use-value in the job market and to a complete divorce of pedagogical concerns from cultural politics. In most media education programs the concerns of the liberal arts are tacked on as a "theoretical" area, resulting in the schizophrenia experienced by both faculty and students. Faculty are split between their roles in industry and academia, and students' lives are divided between their roles as producers and consumers. These splits are the result of and impetus for a separation of theory from practice. The ultimate outcome is a depoliticized pedagogy that has lost any notion of education as a site for public sphere activity aimed at furthering the goals of a radical democracy.

Added to this is media education's dead-end attempt to define itself as a discipline. To say that media education should not be a discipline is to call attention to the fracturing of knowledge forms in postmodernism, but it is not to say that media education should simply be a hodgepodge of other disciplines. Instead, we need to conceive of media education's interdisciplinarity as existing within a postdiscipline, one in which the rigid walls of disciplinarity are replaced with bridges. Media education, then, must reject two forms of discipline, the discipline of industrial modes of training and the discipline of the traditional university structure where the boundaries of fields serve to shut off the thoughts of educators within narrowly defined and standardized departments.

Given our critique of media education, we can propose two levels of solution for establishing a new direction for our area of pedagogy. The first level is on a grand scale—a utopian project of reconstructing the entire educational system, requiring in the first place an overall social transformation. This solution requires an ever diligent moral critique of the conditions and practices of late capitalism and the cultural conservatism that carries these practices forward in the service of a total denigration of democracy. Such a solution can only be utopian, and within the present decline of American democracy, this future-directed project seems futile and impractical. But we believe that looking toward and calling for such a utopian dream is not just an exercise in far-fetched, ivory tower isolationism. Although the impossibility, at present, of such a transformation must be practically dealt with, the imagining of a better future can channel our efforts in the present toward vital alternatives. The utopian moment makes it possible to conceptualize and effectively encounter those formations in social history that really do make a difference in the construction of our political and cultural institutions.

This practice connects with Foucault's development of a genealogical practice that "transforms history from a judgement on the past in the name of the present truth to a counter-memory that combats our current modes of truth and justice, helping us to understand and change the present by placing it in relation to the past [and to the future]" (Arac, 1986, xviii). Thus, a utopian project is not just future-directed, it draws upon the struggles of the past that have challenged and in part transformed historical conditions. It is through this kind of practice that the Left can confront the Right's pedagogical strategies directly, for the struggles surrounding the uncovering of these countermemories are actually about a real fight—a fight over popular memory. The present apparatus of political and pedagogical control has set up an array of practices that obstruct the flow of popular memory.

Since memory is actually a very important factor in struggle (really, in fact, struggles develop in a kind of conscious moving forward of history), if one controls people's memory, one controls their dynamism. And one also controls their experience, their knowledge of previous struggles. (Foucault, 1989, 92)

Intellectuals must take up this struggle by being "bearers of dangerous memory" (Giroux, 1988, 99), keeping alive the memory of human suffering and attempts (successful and unsuccessful) to overcome that suffering. These struggles are not about abstract conceptualizations of the motion of history, but are rooted in the popular imagination. The possibilities for reactivating an effective project for emancipatory cultural politics are not waiting to be found, they are already present in the popular memory—in the subjugated knowledges, local narratives, resistances, and traditions of specific and diverse struggles over everyday life.

This broader project, which we leave at this moment, must serve as the basis for the second level of solution—a positive pragmatic approach that takes steps within the present conditions. We will focus on this level of solution in the remainder of this chapter and in the next. This is not to say that the solutions to media education's problems within present conditions should be carried forward strictly pragmatically with no conception of a utopian alternative. However, our focus needs to be on how we can change the present structure and conditions of media education in order both to do what we can do now, and to open up possibilities for a more radical transformation.

The solutions we offer are partial and open; they are pragmatic steps toward overcoming the problems in media education that we have de-scribed. Our critique has led us to see that the discourse and practice of media education is fundamentally dichotomized around the pairs profes-sional/liberal arts, producer/consumer, teacher/student, work/culture, and so on. We believe this schizophrenic discourse is principally centered in the opposition between theory and practice, and the solutions we will offer are aimed squarely at overcoming this founding dichotomy. Before suggesting the concrete things that can be done, we need to look at the antecedent pedagogical conditions that circumscribe the possibilities for change in media education.

ANTECEDENT PEDAGOGICAL CONDITIONS

The problems in university education will persist unless there is change at a more fundamental level across the entire educational system. Pedagogy at the university level is faced with its own problems, but also with the problems inherited from elementary and secondary education. It would indeed be a false utopia to believe that simply adopting an alternative pedagogical scheme at the university could reverse all of the problems students have faced in their educational history. The general problems in pedagogy in K–12 are simply too large and too diverse to cover in any detail here, but we believe there are some general conditions that need to be addressed. These problems need to be overcome at the K–12 level if a critical pedagogy at the university level is ever to come to full fruition. But we also need to understand these problems, now, as the background with which we have to work.

A primary problem in K–12 is that the pedagogical situation is constructed as a motivational game in which the teacher stands in for or develops the student's subjectivity, while the student passively receives both a subject position and an objective content of knowledge. Students do not passively accept information from the authoritative pedagogue, rather they are ingrafted into a more fundamental form of passivity—one in which they refuse to take responsibility for their own education. Instead, they compliantly sit back and wait to be motivated by the teacher. There are a number of factors in the educational system that lead to this situation: education is separated from life; classrooms are setup into rigid patterns; classes are divided up into abstract "subjects"; pedagogy takes predominantly a banking approach; the practices that knowledge applies to are held off in a distant future of adulthood; teachers set up a false authority for themselves through withholding any knowledge of the context of educational practice; success and "achievement" are expressed in grades as markers of competitive prowess; and so on.

In this educational environment there is little chance that the student will develop the motivation to learn, that is, as an internal condition of empowerment. Typically, students resist the authority of the teacher and reject the imposition of knowledge through rote learning. The successful teacher is the one who can motivate the students to learn, but this practice of motivation is one that is wholly carried out by the teacher. Through exciting presentation, humor and entertainment, the teacher can inspire the students to take an interest in the subject material. However, when the students go on to the next teacher, they sit and wait for motivation to come. They have not developed the motivation to learn, they have had motivation done to them.

In such a condition, students acquiesce and become passive subjects who are taught that education is something that comes to you. These are the same students who come into the media education classroom at the university. They have incorporated a stance in which they have silenced their own voices and wait, once again, for the professor to give them the things they will need for their careers. The result is that the parcelling out of facts in an entertaining way becomes the model of what good college teaching is about. This model of education fits well with the professional training approach. Of course, the entertainer teacher, who goes to no ends to pry out motivation from the students, is considered successful. But neither of these models of pedagogy has anything to do with empowering students to explore their own lives, to draw upon their experience and knowledge, to connect their education with political practice, or to be critical and active citizens in a democracy. In order for a critical pedagogy to come about these disempowering practices must be reversed.

The task for media education in the university is to reintegrate theory and practice, and this will ultimately require beginning the task in K–12. Seeing education as cultural politics is not something that begins in college. We need to overcome the current practices of K–12: the standardization of the curriculum through the imposition of textbooks that objectify knowledge and history, and shun the advance of critical reflection and multicultural concerns; the normalizing discipline of the educational experience in which issues of race, class and gender are erased and/or submerged in a pro-capitalist liberal pluralism; the reduction of education to schooling through the back to basics approach, in which pedagogy is reduced to increasing cognitive capacities, honing work skills, developing literacy or memorizing a body of "neutral" knowledge for personal development; the production of the American citizen as reciter of the merits of an unshackled capitalism and upholder of "sacred" national values; and so forth.

All of these practices work to undermine critical reflection and to separate education into two spheres—one that is practical, concrete and "will get you ahead," and one that is theoretical, abstract and "overly intellectual." The schizophrenia we experience in media education starts at this early level. The practice of connecting education to citizenship, of seeing the political and cultural implications of our practices, of acquiring knowledge about the social forms through which human beings live, need to begin at the K–12 level. For our purposes, this rethinking of education should include thinking about the media and its impact on students' lives.

As opposed to England, Scotland, and other Western democracies, which have fairly highly developed programs of media study in early education, this country has no developed program of media study at the K–12 level. Given that American media are the most highly developed in the world, this lack of attention to its study is appalling. We seem to think that children learn about the media here by watching it. From a very early age students learn that media and all the other areas of popular culture are separate from education and have very little place in it. We are sure that they should learn the Constitution, develop the ability to discern "good" literature, but as to the media, "let them watch commercials." Not only are basic knowledge of media criticism and how our media work shunned, the use of popular culture in examining political, cultural and economic subject areas is severely limited. In order to put media education on its feet in the university, that is, to see it develop into a valid area of inquiry and practice, we need to overturn the lack of attention to media study at all levels of education.

Another set of antecedent pedagogic conditions with which we must deal are those that are centered around the university as a whole. We have already discussed the conditions in terms of the discourse of the liberal arts, but we need to understand some further conditions in which we presently have to work. These conditions include antidemocratic decision making, political constraints and economic effects on pedagogy.

Often, we in media education are faced with two types of antidemocratic constraints: a low position of influence on university policies and priorities due to a number of factors, including communication's low status among the disciplines; and a general, internal management style that precludes establishing any kind of collective spirit of democratic action. Universities, far from being the open and democratic institutions that educational theory supposes them to be, are run as businesses by business people for business. Pedagogical concerns take a back seat to overall efficiency, economic mandates, bureaucratic methods of control and fund-raising. Universities obviously must exercise fiscal responsibility, but it is now the case that budgets, state and federal funds, and industry tie-ins are such dominant concerns that they drive pedagogy. At the present time, we are faced with this mode of operation; only a steady critique of these practices and a piecemeal implementation of small-scale gains are possible at the present time.

Media education is in a particularly bad position at many universities (particularly, in non-Ph.D.-granting schools) due to its low status among divisions in the university. The authors have worked in a variety of institutions where communication departments were in a constant state of reassessment by the schools and university administration. In addition, administrators have little understanding of the expense of operating any kind of media facility, and funds are always hard to come by unless industry connections are installed. Finally, professionally driven media departments are ones where primary research is given short shrift and teaching loads are often high, thus leading to difficulties for faculty in promotion and tenure. Again, these burdens of low status and economic hardship are factors that we currently have to live with.

Within media education departments the persistent problem of pedagogical versus administrative modes of decision making significantly undermines the practice of democracy in departments. We are faced with the common situation where administrators within our departments bracket pedagogical concerns in favor of fitting into the general mode of operation of management that colors university administration. The result is that decision making functions under a false democracy in which final power is centered in the back rooms of department chairs and deans. Many chairs operate in a mode of divide and conquer, pitting the faculty against each other and withholding/giving out information in such a manner that people on the faculty conceive of themselves as individuals, not as a faculty as a whole. Where individual chairs attempt to keep pedagogy as a high priority and attempt to implement a fair democracy, they are often met with insurmountable pressures from above that tend to steer them toward instrumental decisions dictated by the businesslike structure of university practice. Overcoming these conditions will require that faculty pull together and support the hiring and practices of chairs who put pedagogy first.

A second constraint on the development of a critical pedagogy in media education is the general economic hardship of universities at the present time. Currently, universities are experiencing hard economic times in which budgets dictate pedagogy: research funding is curbed, equipment purchases are cut back, faculty are given higher teaching loads, class sizes increase, departments are evaluated in cost-benefit terms. These conditions cannot be completely overcome at the present time. Yes, individual departments can seek outside funding, but this will often tie them to an industry training approach. The solutions to these problems will require a new level of commitment to education that was not in evidence from George Bush, our self-proclaimed "education president." Nor have our "education governors" or the current Clinton administration addressed the issues in a manner significantly different from Bush's "America 2000," a plan steeped in patriotism and technocracy.

Finally, political constraints exist at the present moment that will constantly steer education toward the professional, instrumental approach. The present conservative climate, with its calls for education as economic development and a back to basics approach, is not conducive to the development of education as a cultural politics. Questioning the sources of economic power in the media, criticizing its ties to conservative politics and developing alternative and multicultural production of media are not the kinds of practices that the present political climate is apt to support. Overcoming these constraints will again require a sustained attack in support of an opening of politics in the university, which will depend on reinvigorating the university as a site of liberating, democratic education.

DEVELOPING A POSTDISCIPLINE

Pragmatic Assumptions

Panoptic Management and Docile Faculty

In order to develop an alternative media education based in the critical pedagogy we have supported we will have to be fully aware of the conditions in which we operate. What are the possibilities? What pragmatic assumptions do we have to make? We would like to address some of these pragmatic conditions in the academy by way of describing the concrete problems currently affecting public higher education, and we will do so by way of example, presenting an analysis of our own institutional experience.[1] We will address the following issues: (1) economic constraints on pedagogy, (2) administration versus faculty as labor, (3) the behaviors of faculty in response to the constraints of state and administrative pressures, (4) the possibilities of resisting these pressures.

In Foucault's *Discipline and Punish* (1979), he attends to "the means of correct training," contending that modern systems of power work to discipline by producing "docile bodies" (docile comes from the Latin root, "teachable"). The practices of training bring together the exercise of power and the constitution of knowledge, in the organization of space and time along ordered lines, so as to facilitate constant forms of surveillance and the operation of evaluation and judgment. The metaphor Foucault employs to capture this discipline is the panopticon, the all-seeing eye of a surveillance that is also a judgment, which does not even have to be looking to make one feel watched.

The state of Ohio, like so many in the United States, has transformed itself into a panopticon. This transformation has taken place through the adoption of managerial/bureaucratic techniques of control. Criteria of efficiency, cohort testing, monitoring and performance comparison are now standard modes of control of faculty. Such managerial methods are what Foucault calls a "moral technology," again metaphorically reproducing the panoptic site; for once management is accepted by the workers (faculty), they have in effect abdicated from any question of, or resistance to, their domination. In this form of management, power is not totally entrusted to someone above, but is acted out by everyone in the institution.

We can see this panopticon operating in the concrete case of the state of Ohio in 1990–93. Here, we have a governor who ran as the "education governor." His first act was to cut the higher education budget by $40 million. Faced with a further budget crisis in the state (of course due to the slashing of social and educational programs by the "education president") the governor of Ohio cut an additional $300 million. This effectively devastated the higher education system. At all of the state campuses the cuts resulted in forced early retirements, firings, a total hiring freeze, increased class sizes, and the eradication of entire departments.

The governor responded to the situation by saying:

The professors are going to have to work harder and smarter and do more with less. If I were the President of a university, I would do what the Japanese do when they don't get what they want. They put black arm bands on and work hard to prove they are deserving. The Board of Regents and our universities are going to have to do it. If they do, they have me out in front. If they don't, they will go at it alone. ("The Governor's Response," 1992, 4)

The governor and the legislators sit in judgment on the universities with copies of Charles T. Sykes's *ProfScam* (1990) on their desks.[2] Their answers to the crisis of higher education: beef up the panopticon, through assembly-line teaching, bigger class loads, cuts in research, reductions of "redundant" programs, turning over more control to industry through ties with corporations, putting the screws to administration and inducing them to put the screws to faculty, conducting efficiency studies and eliminating "nonproductive" courses (meaning anything critical or resistant).

Thus, the state, and in reaction, the administration of the universities, have put fear into our hearts, inducing a discipline on our hearts and souls. Like the prisoners in Bentham's Panopticon we don't know if we are being watched, but are sure that we might be. Thus, outward control becomes secondary, we have become the principle of our own subjection.

As the dictates come down from above, the faculty reacts with immediate accommodation. Our reaction is one of fear and passivity. For instance, the calls for increased teaching loads are unofficial at this point, yet, one state-funded communication department instituted an increase of 30 percent in order "to look like team players to the administration." Through this action they hoped to fend off a cut of their program. Such a response amounts to a total denigration of pedagogy and the worth of education. Yet, this is the prototypical response: act with the power, so as not to lose your place. Docile bodies, corrupted souls.

For individual faculty, tenure is of course a primary worry. How far will one go to assure getting it? One faculty member stated, "I'll teach 150 students in my production class if I have to" (this class currently has 15 students). Thus, we see how the panopticon normalizes as it disciplines. How is one to carry out concerns with critical pedagogy and liberating education under such conditions? From within the panoptic tenure process the only answer is to accommodate.

What are the rewards for critical pedagogy? An example: Two faculty produced a document that proposed a video production pedagogy based on a mildly critical model. The plan would involve increasing student access to equipment by 300 percent by eliminating the remote van that is used for football and other sports production. Most faculty in the department reacted by calling the document "chilling and uncollegial," or by saying, "But if we do that the administration won't like it." Instead of holding firm against the administration, instead of debating the pedagogical issues, instead of proving the validity of this educational practice to the higher-ups, most of the faculty reacted in a hostile manner to the authors. The final result—the department chair dictated, supposedly in accord with the president's dictate, that the department will do football forever, period.

But is this really the only response—bow down to the pressures of the chair, court the rich alumni, no matter what the pedagogical stakes, acquiesce to the presidents? The documents was never discussed; the faculty never attempted to present a different case to the dean or anyone; the students were never asked what they wanted; and the two authors were, for awhile, asked to apologize and then simply to shut up.

What possible actions can we take against the types of disciplinary managerial control fostered by the current institution? First of all, refusal. We can simply refuse to do what the managerial bureaucrats ask. Don't fill out the efficiency reports, don't increase class size, don't do football, don't give up research, don't turn in your peers, don't accommodate, take the consequences. Such actions can have devastating consequences, such as plain old dismissal, but perhaps reequipping the docile body with some muscle can create new spaces. Now, this refusal, properly equipped, needs to be connected with strategies that undermine the control of the panoptic gaze: these refusals need to be backed by student support, and their parents' support, by well-argued position papers, by tenured peers in various locations in the university, by legislators who have been won over by faculty action, and so forth.

Thus, to carry out the refusal we need to be active in protest and we need to break down the normalizing gaze that works to stall protest by both students and faculty. We need to be for and with students and help them to be with and for us—to stand firm in support of our mutual interests.

Second, we need to push for faculty unionization. The current budget cuts and governmental animosity toward faculty makes this more of a possibility today. Many conservative faculty who have stood against organization may be ready to rehear the arguments. Unions need to expand their functions by organizing support groups in the university. Tenured faculty need to be available as advisors for untenured faculty and need to be willing to stand up for them. All faculty need to lend their expertise in various matters to others. For instance, faculty who have been reprimanded for political action need to advise those who are putting themselves in the same position; faculty who have endured the tenure war, need to help those who are currently doing battle.

These possibilities for resistance offer some hope that the panoptic effect can be reversed, giving us back our souls and bodies.

Fragmentation: Media Education as Grab Bag

We must also attend to the pragmatic condition of the fragmentation of areas of knowledge within the university as a whole and within media departments. The structure of universities into divisions, schools, colleges and departments has had adverse effects on developing a coherent approach to media education. As we noted in chapter 3, media studies exists within and across a number of diverse institutional arrangements at different universities. This has resulted in a "homelessness" for the study of mass communication, as it continually deals with the problems of being placed within departments that deal with any number of fragmented fields of inquiry and practice, such as theater, speech communication, speech audiology, journalism, audio/visual arts, telecommunication, and so on.

The incoherent fragmentation and specialization of disciplines in the university as a whole is most acute in the area of media studies. Media studies takes on the flavor of whatever institutional arrangement it is thrown into: if placed in the social sciences it tends to replicate the dominant paradigm of quantitative effects theory; if placed in the humanities it tends to model itself on English, with an even stronger tendency to separate theoretical and critical course work from "practical" course work; if it is situated in a professional school it inherits the models of industry specialization that fragment it into debilitating areas of management, journalism, general studies and production.

Not only are media studies departments fragmented through university-wide arrangements, they are internally divided by incoherent curricular structures that preclude an approach that would allow the critical assessment of large-scale political and cultural conditions of the media. The typical department organizes itself around an assortment of unconnected goals and curricular arrangements. The failure of media education to acquire the status of a discipline or even a coherent interdisciplinary matrix is part and parcel of this debilitating fragmentation. Curricula are divided up into diverse tracks such as media management, media journalism, media technology, media production, media performance, media criticism, media policy and law, and so on. The tracking system leads students to see themselves as focused on a specific track, and to see the other areas of inquiry as secondary and in many cases useless. Faculty are hired into various specialties defined by the tracks, resulting in factional groups that have no view of the department as a whole.

This situation is one in which the department never comes to any sense of community; instead, faculty in the various areas war against each other. Both students and faculty are isolated into alienated factions that pursue their various goals, often at odds with others who could instead be allies. The possibilities for political and cultural debate, for opening up questions of difference in considering the contemporary politics of multiculturalism, and for students and faculty to work within a community that strives to see the educational situation as aimed at developing democratic citizenship skills are virtually shut down by this fragmented condition.

We must accept that these problems will persist, but should at the same time strive to create the type of institutional arrangements that can make a critical pedagogy possible. This means proposing and fighting for media education as a valid area of inquiry and refusing the kind of institutional arrangements that are imposed merely out of expediency. It means working for curricula that reintegrate the fragmented tracks of contemporary departments. And it means striving for a sense of community within departments, encouraging the kind of interdisciplinarity that encourages coherence and at the same time fosters critical debate between our now isolated factions.

Things We Can Do Now

Even given the constraints of the current condition of education in the United States, there are definitely a number of things we can do to reorient media education in the university. Yes, restructuring our departments will take hard work and we will in most cases have to be content with changes that do not go all the way toward a critical media education. But our hopes for a better practice of media education should become a force for change, a fortifier of our will and a support for democratic practices.

Transforming Graduate Education

A first step in the right direction is to take the very issues we have been discussing and address them in programs of media graduate education. As we have noted, current graduate education in mass communication and media studies works to create the schizophrenia we encounter as faculty by instituting a separation of theory and practice. Graduate students study the media in isolation from their jobs as teaching assistants, where they teach by rote and train undergraduates in dominant practices. We can recall little in our own graduate educations that would prepare us for the real world of academia with its schizophrenia, politics and undertheorized pedagogy. Most graduate programs do not address pedagogy at all, and if they do, they address only teaching practices, that is, skills for how to teach. The first thing we can do is change this condition right now.

We need to develop a graduate education in our field that directly addresses the nature of pedagogy in the university, the conflicts in the academy, the current problems in the field of media education, critical pedagogic applications to our field, the cultural politics of university education, the pragmatic and not so pragmatic routines and procedures of the media department and, most important, the separation of theory and practice that weighs so heavily upon us. In this manner, we can insure that the future faculty in our field will have at least been exposed to the problems we have been addressing.

First, graduate education can and often does provide the type of community that is usually lacking in media undergraduate departments. Graduate students (future faculty) share offices, engage in debate, take common courses, discuss teaching assignments, form personal relationships with fellow students and faculty and engage in active contestation over the particularities of the field. This community can be bolstered by encouraging active debate over the nature of pedagogy. This community can be expanded by: providing pedagogic mentors for graduate students, offering course work in the issues of media education, putting on mini-conferences where outside faculty and students address issues in media education and by providing guidelines for how graduate students can implement these pedagogic concerns in their programs.

Pedagogy must become a part of the curriculum of graduate media education. First of all, graduate students should be introduced to the diverse and contestatory history of media studies in such a way that they actively attempt to make connections with all of the areas of the field, instead of being pigeonholed into their fragmented domains of research. Graduate education, of all places, should be the type of democratic public sphere where the fractures and debates in the field are approached as significant practices that connect to broader political, economic and cultural problems. Graduate students must be forced to ask the big questions, and this can be done through introductory and continuing courses that address the important issues in the field from a variety of theoretical positions. An active questioning of what media education is and where it is going should be encouraged through integrating such concerns into all course work and studies.

Further, faculty can provide graduate students with insight into the practice of education by not simply focusing on getting courses taught, but by constantly prodding students to address pedagogical issues. There are several practical ways in which this can be accomplished. First, when students take courses in disciplines outside the field, they can be asked to attend to the pedagogic problems in that particular field, even producing reports for the media faculty. Second, course work in other fields such as educational leadership, critical legal studies, women's studies and critical pedagogy can be suggested to students as part of their program. All of these fields have courses that address some of the issues we have been discussing. Third, students should be required to assess the pedagogic issues involved in their own teaching practices. Finally, students should be required to think about how their own work, practical and especially theoretical, connects with what they are doing in the classroom. Faculty should ask graduate students to incorporate what they are learning in their theory, methodology and history courses into their undergraduate teaching. This can be accomplished even in courses such as video production that seem at first sight detached from Q-sorts, audience surveys, the history of technology, or cultural studies. However, questions in these theoretical and methodological areas are pertinent. If connections cannot be made then something is wrong with the way in which the production course is being taught.

All of these practices can be implemented right now in our graduate programs. The result may be a graduate education that starts the process of critical pedagogy: overcoming the theory/practice split, calling attention to how research connects with teaching, tuning in the future faculty to the kinds of pedagogical concerns that will constrain or liberate them in their careers as media educators.

Addressing Pedagogy within Undergraduate Education

We can also begin the process of foregrounding pedagogy in the undergraduate classroom. This can be done now, by implementing a practice that radicalizes Graff's notion of "teaching the conflicts" (1992). In current media pedagogy we work to erase the workings of pedagogy in the classroom, attempting to make teaching and learning seem a natural thing that lies outside the knowledge of the student. How often do we address our own teaching practices with students, how often do we ask students to think about the goals of the course and question them, how often do we bring criticism to bear at the very moment of pedagogy?

Jerry Herron (1988, 137–38) offers a number of useful suggestions: (1) invite students to write about what they do/don't like about the university and the department, and discuss it with them; (2) each fall, stage a colloquium for incoming students and address why particular classes matter; (3) make copies of the statements of purpose of your university and explain to your students why you agree or disagree with it; (4) make a list of your intellectual adversaries and explain to your students who they are and why you disagree with them; (5) ask the students to make a list of things they would rather be doing, do the same yourself and discuss the lists.

These suggestions may seem humorous at first, and these are not perhaps the particular practices that should be employed. However, what they do is put pedagogy out on the table. There is no better way to get students taking education seriously than to take it seriously yourself, and this means going out on a limb by making your own pedagogy visible, warts and all. We think that Herron's suggestions and other similar practices would serve to open up the classroom and begin the slow process of turning students' attention to their own responsibility in their education.

We suggest one further practice along these lines—talk and talk about theory and practice. Each day in class come up with a couple of examples of how an esoteric study you read or a theory you reflected on has a real bearing on something that actually concerns students. If you can't, then either you have no understanding of your students' everyday concerns or you are reading the wrong esoteric essays. For example, in an audio class a question about rap music arose. Wasn't it amateurish to rely on simply playing around with a turntable? Who would let us do this when we get jobs? Isn't this really just botching up a slip cue? The instructor had been reading an article by a cultural studies scholar on rap music as a cultural phenomenon. It struck him that the use of the turntable by rap was a postmodern inflection of the modernist movement in art where the attempt was to rethink the tools, making the familiar strange. In rap, the turntable is perceived and lived differently—no longer is it simply a playback device designed to reproduce the sounds of commodities, rather it is seen as a musical instrument. Thus, rap's use of the turntable is not simply a reuse of a technology, it is a political reworking of a technology, turning a passive reproductive device into an active instrument controlled by and for the black community. Such an account sheds light on the students' questions, asking them to consider the political implications of the technology they use and to consider how what is given as a broadcast industry tool can be used differently for alternative purposes.

This example illustrates one way in which our lives as theorists can be integrated with our lives in the classrooms, and how student's lives as producers and consumers can be connected. We leave it to each faculty member to explore methods within their own context in which theory and practice come together in a manner that aids students to explore the practical, political and cultural ramifications of what they learn and do.

Building a Critical Media Curriculum: Theory and Practice

At the undergraduate level, media education has shortchanged a pedagogy of cultural politics, ignoring education as a way of developing citizenship skills and knowledge. Instead, professionalism has held sway, separating student's lives into roles of producer and consumer. A reworked media education must reintegrate our lives by focusing on how social, political and cultural practices and theories bear upon the practice of producing the media.

We want now to make some suggestions for how our conception of a critical pedagogy can be implemented. Fundamental to this project is the development of a curriculum that reintegrates theory and practice. As we have noted, this is not a matter of simply teaching courses in both theory and practical training, nor is it simply a matter of bringing some theory into the practical courses. Instead, we must annihilate the very distinction—all of our courses should be theoretical-practical. In carrying out this task we need to keep in mind the three areas of inquiry suggested by critical pedagogy's reflection on popular culture (see chapter 1). First, how can popular culture be taken up in the classroom in a manner in which it both gives validity to student experiences and interrogates those experiences in relation to cultural politics? Second, how can popular culture itself be engaged as pedagogical? Third, how should we conceive our own pedagogical practice in dealing with popular culture?

The first area suggests that we turn our attention to those forms of media that are instrumental and significant to students—rock 'n roll, music television, the new young adult cartoons, comic books, youth films, soap opera, and so on. By turning our attention here, we can tap the underlying political and cultural knowledge that students already have, and use these genres as ways of exploring political economy, cultural politics and audience meaning-making. Of course, the genres students reject are no less important, and we can also strive to develop students' understanding of and interest in "serious" narrative film, documentary and news. But instead of excluding the popular from our "serious" courses on high drama, broadcast news, and so on, we should strive to show how it is interconnected with them.

The second area of inquiry suggests that we integrate pedagogical concerns directly into the curriculum. If media are pedagogical machines, then we can draw out the educational significance of political and cultural knowledge forms, using the media's pedagogy as a springboard to heighten students' awareness of their own responsibility in dealing with educational influences. Finally, the third area suggests a practice of constant criticism, a criticism that opens up the realm of practice. Our courses should continually raise questions of social responsibility and democratic citizenship and put this questioning to the test in practical work.

We need to remodel our curriculum in light of these concerns. To begin, we need to throw out all our past syllabi and curricular statements and start from scratch. As an experiment the faculty could institute a set a guidelines for rethinking the curriculum: (1) any course you design cannot have a title that is currently in use; (2) any course you design cannot have the word broadcast in it; (3) any course you design must include something that students must do—an activity that connects with actual political, economic, aesthetic or cultural practices; (4) any course you design must include a statement for the students on why you want to teach the course. The resulting courses would probably be a hellishly unconnected mishmash, but it would probably also be, in many ways, better than the present curriculum. Of course, we need to be more attuned to the overall goals of the curriculum in setting up its purposes, areas of inquiry, requirements, sequences, and so on. We will attempt to develop some ideas for a specific curriculum in the final chapter.

The remodeling of the curriculum must proceed from the fundamental philosophical position that media studies is an area of inquiry, not a job track. The proclivity to conceive of the media major as job area should be nipped in the bud. Students should see the curriculum as fundamentally concerned with studying the media, and this should not be disconnected from doing it. It would be ultimately helpful to ask students to erase from their minds what they want to do in the media as they begin their program of study. They should instead learn what it is they can do at the end of their studies. The curriculum, in itself, can help this along by eliminating references to job tracks, separate practical areas, and so forth. One of the great absurdities of media departments is that we ask our students to choose a track of employment at the beginning of their second year, when they have very little knowledge of what the choices are. In addition, by putting out theoretical and criticism courses in the senior year, we preclude students from considering the political and cultural implications of their employment choices. We propose a hard and fast rule—no job tracks.

Whatever form the curriculum takes, it should be fundamentally concerned with the primacy of the media as a public sphere that impacts the workings of democracy. This means that students should be learning how media produces meaning, how those meanings are inflected by citizen-viewers and how the practice of doing media is always a political/cultural act. The "product" of our programs should not be media workers, it should be citizen-viewers, citizen-producers, citizen-media critics.

New Kinds of Work

A curriculum of media education aimed at developing understanding of the media and media practice as social, political, cultural phenomenon needs to expand its conception of what work is. We need to develop possibilities for practicum work in a broad range of media industries and outlets. By forging connections with the broadcast industries, advertising agencies, local broadcast news stations and university sports complexes, we have severely limited our students' access to the kind of broad inquiry they need. We should provide the opportunities for students to experience some of these industries, but they should also be exposed to public access centers, community action groups, broad-based arts coalitions, alternative forms of media, educational media and other types of nonbroadcast media.

Exposure to the industry through internships, courses that set up productions for clients, cable practicums and other work outside the confines of classes should be offered. However, these experiences, too, should be conceptualized as critical adventures that have a significant theoretical component to them. Simply sending students out into the media industry to take part in internships, where they become ingrafted into the rules of the game and are swept up in the "glamour" of "the way they really do it," is detrimental to a critical pedagogy. Experiences outside the classroom should require the same kind of theoretical-practical coupling that a course in media and society would give. Students should be required to work on papers and journals that connect to their internships and other media productions.

Again, fundamental pedagogical goals must come first. Do we want to simply provide cheap labor to the broadcast industry and reproduce a work-force for the dominant media, or do we want to educate students to see the media as an important public sphere, where race, gender and class issues need to be significantly addressed? The work students do must address these issues; the kind of work we presently engage them in is often closed from any considerations of how the media may be changed, how its deficiencies may be overcome.

On the other hand, we are not recommending simply turning media studies into a theoretical game disconnected from practice. There is certainly a need to reconceive the field of media studies as a postdiscipline that focuses on the theoretical, methodological, historical and critical understanding of the media. However, this development of the field as one of inquiry must avoid a narrow intellectual approach detached from practice. As Aronowitz (1989, 201) states, "There can be no cultural pedagogy without a cultural practice." A strictly intellectual take on the media abrogates the responsibility to take part in transforming the public sphere into a site for the development of a radical democracy.

We need, then, to transform our own work into the kind of engaged practice that serves as an example for our students and for media workers in general. Disciplined scholarship in the theoretical and methodological high ground is certainly necessary, but we also need to connect our own work to practices that circulate into wider arenas. Intellectuals need to come out of the academy and make connections with the greater community. Critical media educators must move beyond the confines of the classroom and into new interrelations with the various new technologies of LPTV (Low Power-Television), public access, community radio, and so on, and with the various community action, environmental, labor, reproductive rights and gay/lesbian groups who currently use these new media technologies.

As this occurs, notions of media literacy extend beyond critical viewing and into the creation of new media forms—forms of media practice—vital components in the counterhegemony. To further connect this to Freire's groundbreaking *Pedagogy of the Oppressed* (1989), media educators, in their own privileged positions in terms of race, class and gender, must (as, in Freire's terms, oppressors at least in terms of their untransformed consciousness) undergo their own transformations of consciousness. And their pedagogy must result inevitably in the continued education of the oppressed by the oppressed. Critical media literacy must work to achieve

modes of presentation, imaging, entertainment and argument that are realizations of collective desires, group aspirations, common projects, shared experience, at the same time that they refuse all ideas—all expression—of standing in for and subsuming the heterogeneous individual-sociality/social-individuality of the actual lives of actual men and women. (Heath, 1990, 298)

CONCLUSION

Given the existing social formation, the modes of communication are operated predominantly in the interests of oppression. This is not a simple mechanical operation but is tied to the hegemonic conjuncture of market, military and political interests. Within this grouping of interests the media serve to construct consensus and dissensus, to reconfigure the relationship of meaning and affect in the construction of a narrative of nation, to surveil the population and in so doing create systems of normalization and subjectification. The contemporary popular media fragments, threatens or erases the practical base of knowledge that marginal or powerless groups need in order to take hold of their everyday lives and work toward changing their historical conditions. And the state of media education within the contemporary U.S. university tends to function as an acritical training ground complicit (at the very least) in an ongoing program of mediated cultural reproduction rather than work toward the kind of linking and bridging within a critical pedagogy of media praxis imagined by Alvarado:

For our purposes today, such distinctions [as those drawn between "theoretical" and "practical"] don't help our understanding of "The Place and Purpose of Media Education. . . ." What I am indicating here is that, at its best, Media Education involves work on the *symbolic*, media *content*, and *practical work*, together with work on areas which I initially identified as being important, i.e., work on the personal, the social, the economic, the political, the institutional and the contemporary. (1990, 3)

The operation of the media is not a seamless operation closing off all possibilities of alternative use. As media educators we can encourage these possibilities by enabling students to become media literate. Remaking media education into such a value-sensitive pedagogical terrain will require that we not shun the struggle over values. The practices we have outlined work toward such a project of infusing critical, political, cultural and value questions into the mass communication curriculum. We can now attempt to flesh out this potential by concretizing what a critical pedagogical media education might look like.

NOTES

1. At this writing, public institutions of higher education are facing a general budget crisis brought on by the general economic crunch and specific cuts in education carried out during the Reagan-Bush years. Our own particular experiences are with the state systems in Indiana and Ohio. The analysis in this section is based on our particular experiences in these settings; however, this personal experience is quite typical, as supported by conversations with colleagues in a variety of institutions across the country.

2. Sykes's argument is particularly effective because it is based in partial truths (the professoriate is riddled with slackers, research is often overemphasized, etc.). The legislature, however, takes this kind of common sense attack as the whole truth and ignores the political ramifications of Sykes's position. As a result, we have legislatures proposing that laws be passed that require faculty to teach five courses a semester, put in eight-hour days and at the same time take cuts in pay.

Part Three:

Toward a Critical Media Pedagogy

Chapter Six

The Theory and Practice of Media Curricula

INTRODUCTION

In the preceding chapters we have examined a critical theory of education in light of its possible contribution to the restructuring of mass communication as an intellectual territory within the contemporary U.S. university. We have begun to construct a bridge connecting these theoretical bodies and, from this vantage point, have outlined a critical pedagogy of media studies.

Mass communication as a territory within the contemporary U.S. university developed within a set of assumptions and relations regarding the various media industries. In the past decade and a half, the slow absorption of critical scholarship from the adjacent literatures of political science, literary studies, film studies and related areas has brought forth a body of critical media scholarship at odds with the more traditional relationship between academia and the media industries. This separation has resulted in tensions in the media studies literature that manifest themselves in various ways throughout the discipline and the profession.[1] These separations extend also into university curricula. At the graduate level, programs and tracks in critical and qualitative methods are offered as alternatives to a social science tradition of more "neutral" quantitative methods. In undergraduate curricula, the separation between theory and practice most frequently is contained in the content of upper-division theory classes in which students are asked to examine critically the very practices that the bulk of their major courses have celebrated.

The schizophrenic character of media studies curricula is engendered in the tension between critique and celebration. The schizophrenia of media studies faculty is encouraged in the discrete separation of the production of critical writings directed at confronting the structures and processes of the dominant media, from the reproduction of these dominant structures and processes in the undergraduate classroom. As media educators, the problem at hand is to find new and better ways of connecting our research to our teaching. This challenge, once undertaken, explodes across all the dimensions of our lives and quickly becomes the greater task of shattering the boundaries that we have erected between students and teachers, citizens and leaders—the boundaries that mark off our lives into the separate compartments of theory and practice, and the disassociated domains of the professional, personal and political.

There are few places within the confines of a traditional mass communication curriculum where these tensions are as pronounced, as openly observable, or as on the surface as in the teaching of television production. There is no place within a media studies curriculum that offers a more promising site for the pedagogical integration of a critical theory of media with the critical practice of media education. Our motives in this selection are also clearly rooted in our own personal and professional investment in media production pedagogy, and in the schizophrenia that originates in the struggle to reunite media theory with media practice—the struggle to confront a long-standing tradition of vocational professionalism.

TEACHING TELEVISION

Traditionally, teaching video production has been viewed as a specialized skill that makes media faculty more marketable. While often taught as a basic introduction to the equipment and conventions of mainstream entertainment television (the basic structure of the textbooks that dominate this market), we believe that teaching introductory video production can be done in a manner capable of opening up uncharted territories of student/teacher consciousness: student consciousness, in that the most basic unspoken epistemological assumptions about the meaning of mediated communication may be brought to the surface, examined and challenged; teacher consciousness, in that the further expansion of theory into new modes of analysis and new ways of seeing can better emerge from the dialectic struggles within the critical pedagogical encounter than from the critic working in isolation. Refracted back through the lens of critical pedagogy, it is the very notion of production itself that is transformed, from the bleak grey recitation/reproduction of aesthetic convention into the broader vista of struggle and negotiation in which the production of new knowledge is possible.

The application of critical theory to the media production classroom begins with the recognition that teaching television production is fundamentally a political act. All such instruction involves empowering students to (each from his or her own perspective) represent the world through images, with the further realization that none of these representations is neutral. Perceptions of reality or ways of seeing are based on individual or group experiences in culture. The representations of images in video are also culturally based; they follow guidelines and standardized formats established with specific cultural and economic purposes in mind. If one does not work actively against the canons of visual representation, or at a minimum question them, one is working in support of continuing the existing methods of shaping reality. It is in this manner, then, that the teaching of introductory video production is a political activity that is either in support of, or in opposition to, existing video production standards as established by commercial broadcast industries.

We think it reasonable for a media department to examine its production curriculum in the context of whether the production practices of that curriculum serve to question or challenge the dominant broadcast model, or to reinforce it. In asking these kinds of questions, the assumptions that both underlie the production classes, and possibly undermine more critical curricular efforts, may be brought to the surface and become the focus of faculty discussion and debate.

Traditional Approaches

For historical and economic reasons discussed in previous chapters, communication departments have served as marketing consultants and preprofessional training centers for the communications industries rather than as sites where critical analysis of that system is conducted. In general, academic departments who employ a vocational approach to media education do not share the view that the development of a critical consciousness is a responsibility of higher education. For Paulo Freire (1989), it is through conscientization (that is, the development of a critical consciousness) that people learn to become subjects capable of acting upon and changing the conditions of their world. Further, Freire believes conscientization to be an educational process stifled by contemporary formal education. In the metaphor of the *banking* model of education, in which teachers make *deposits* of *knowledge* into students' brains, there is no place for the production of new knowledge (perhaps analogous to counterfeiting, in keeping with the terms of the metaphor—the unauthorized or unsanctioned production of knowledge).

In the specific context of television production, the difficulty is in opening spaces within the curriculum in which students can discover ways to act upon and change their world. Teachers are frustrated, sad and angry when student productions seem little more than transparent attempts to clone their favorite broadcast entertainment programs. These feelings emanate from the structural impossibility of conscientization, as well as the complicit role played by media faculty in this structure and the impact upon the culture at large of training another generation of polished professional media practitioners. This silent acquiescence of cultural practitioners in both the media and higher education is an important contemporary characteristic of Gramsci's concept of hegemony. Critical pedagogy offers tools for identifying the construction of this hegemonic practice and calling into question the unexamined, unrecognized (and undeniably) political dimension of all areas of media studies.

After a decade or more of teaching basic television production—rotating thousands of students through each piece of production equipment and each studio crew position, employing various exercises modeled on news, sports, talk, comedy and instructional formats, writing uncountable numbers of quizzes and exams based upon the standard glossy large and expensive introductory textbooks—it is not surprising to feel a bit awkward (if not pointedly absurd) in using the phrase "critical consciousness" in the context of writing about basic television production. Critical pedagogy challenges these feelings, asks us to consider the specific constructions of normalcy in contrast to which we stand in embarrassed silence. A critical video pedagogy begins with recognition of the cultural and political nature of education, particularly as it applies to video production and media literacy.

Any approach toward changing the conditions of the video production classroom must begin with the alteration, rethinking or elimination of the structured categorizations that typify the traditional model. Critical practice demands the integration of media production curricula with the analysis and critique of traditional broadcast program models. Such a discussion might select a focus upon the differences in content, technique and construction of the audience between broadcasting and community access, cable and/or video art approaches. Throughout, the crucial element is in the dialectical relationship between student and teacher, a relationship that is particularly difficult in this setting.

For the student, whose entire education has been designed around the autocratic/patriarchal/authoritative principles that characterize primary and secondary education in the United States, breaking from the familiar (even if it is repressive) can trigger a crisis of insecurity. There is an undeniable security in a structure that outlines the territory to be studied and divides knowledge into prearranged segments—understandable, digestible, to be committed to memory and called up upon demand as evidence of under-standing—all with predictable and prearranged results in the form of quantitative evaluation.

For the teacher, whose own formal education has been played out across similar terrain, the surrender of authority results in a similar fall into insecurity. The role of expert (for which graduate school is apprenticeship) must be somehow repositioned or recast to allow for a dialogue whose aim is not fixed, to work toward goals as yet undetermined. For both student and teacher the many predetermined aspects of their relationship offer additional obstacles to be worked through. It is, for example, one thing to suggest that there are no real answers to the questions we will consider, and another thing entirely some time later to pass out exams with irregular blank patches into which the answers must be written.

Critical pedagogy does not simply ask us to be *critical* (in the left political sense of the term). It is possible for critical media theory (feminist theory, critical pedagogy, etc.) to be taught in as repressive a manner as any other subject. Media faculty must avoid working with a hidden agenda that fits their world view of media, and that gives students only the illusion of discovery as the "correct" critical answers are reached according to preestablished structures.

Whether or not direct ties (in the form of internships, scholarships, endowments, etc.) connect an academic program to commercial broadcast industries, production pedagogy remains profoundly influenced by the production industry. This influence is ideological in character, and directs media education toward particular models of production, prescribing a particular model of pedagogy in which professional techniques are repli-cated in the classroom. The problem of compartmentalization of knowledge is particularly prevalent in basic video instruction. First the equipment (cameras, video switchers, lights, etc.) is presented, often with simple production exercises employing the familiar models of news or talk formats. In this way, the established conventions of broadcasting (the "right way" to speak, move a camera, frame a shot, etc.) are presented as normal, reinforc-ing the apolitical facade of dominant entertainment programming. Instead, in keeping with Freire's principles, the discussion is best initiated by screening programs from commercial broadcast and alternative sources. Dominant media products can then be compared with their counterparts in alternative media in a manner that presents neither as *normal*. Furthermore, this discussion ideally takes place before production equipment is approached, so the tools and processes can be placed in the proper perspective. The important point is that having students imitate the *normal* method of video production before letting them explore the *other* production styles serves to legitimize the dominant production method, as well as the educational system that promotes the "tradition."

Throughout the production curriculum, exercises and projects should stress process over product; the method used to arrive at the completed project should be considered as much as, or more than, the project itself. Therefore, exercises that encourage experimentation are important. Further, since by definition most experiments end in failure, it is essential that the concept of failure in this new context be recast as a natural by-product of larger and more important learning (rather than a bad grade).

Overcoming Professionalism

The ideology of professionalism is primarily rooted in certain habits of the mind. Administrators see local TV operations as the logical model of "real" media production and base their expectations of production education accordingly. Production faculty replicate the professional curriculum in which they themselves were trained. And all of this takes place within the greater context of a larger environment in which the university itself is being pulled toward both the needs and the outlook of business. Many communication departments feature courses and programs in which communication is conceived in the same manner in which capitalist business conceives anything: it is a product to be bought and sold, and it need only be understood in its commodity terms, that is, in terms of what makes it more or less salable or profitable. This extremely instrumental approach to communication is then reflected in production courses that present production as a series of tasks to be mastered and rules to be learned by rote.

The alternative is to conceive of communication as a basic, specific human activity, and to offer a curriculum that explores this specificity, that investigates how communication works to create and transmit meaning. Within this approach, production classes would become, in effect, courses in applied semiotics, criticism and analysis. This would place production pedagogy firmly within the traditions and goals of the liberal arts.

Production courses must become part of a larger communication curriculum that addresses the way symbols are created and used within our society. Such a communication curriculum would have as its aim to develop a student's problem-solving skills and critical abilities, applied to communication processes and goals. At the same time, such a communication curriculum would resonate in harmony with the development of these skills and abilities applied throughout a greater arts, humanities and sciences curriculum. Such a resonance would come as a welcome relief to communication faculty accustomed to an attitude of benign patronization from their colleagues in the traditional arts and science disciplines.

Within this curriculum students should develop: (1) knowledge of the sorts of choices available in encoding processes; (2) knowledge of effects or influences these choices hold over decoding processes; (3) the analytical ability to recognize and deal with these choices wisely, both as creators of messages and as respondents. Communication students must understand the ethical and political dimensions of communication practice. In short, communication studies within the liberal arts must understand communication not as a job track, but as a key agent of social relations deserving of intellectual attention, including scientific and philosophical inquiry.

Within this general purpose of communication education, the study of the mass media should play a central role. Gitlin (1980) notes:

The media bring a manufactured public world into private space. From within their private crevices, people find themselves relying on the media for concepts, for images of their heroes, for guiding information, for emotional charges, for a public recognition of values, for symbols in general, even for language. Of all the institutions of daily life, the media specialize in orchestrating everyday consciousness—by virtue of their pervasiveness, their accessibility, their centralized symbolic capacity. They name the world's parts, they certify reality as reality. (1–2)

What names do the media give as they define the world? What language do they speak as they shape the central concepts of our culture? How does the symbolic system work? And who does it work for? What are the institutional determinants of media messages? Under what constraints do media producers work? How do the prevalent symbolic and institutional systems mesh with other systems? How do they mesh with other such social values as democracy, freedom, equality, culture, progress? Should the language of the media be used differently, or changed altogether? Should we seek different institutional arrangements? These are the sorts of questions a mass communication curriculum aimed at critical thinking and value problems must pose.

A critical pedagogy of media studies must insist that these questions pervade and inform all aspects of the curriculum. At the level of programmatic/departmental design, a media studies major must be conceptualized from the outset to intertwine media practice with media theory. At the level of individual course design and implementation, the theoretical analysis of mass media must not be bracketed off into neatly structured (and isolated) courses in which dominant media values are examined and critiqued inside a closed system where any implications of such critique are stored and contained, cut adrift from practical classes in which the business-as-usual practice of media production proceeds behind a facade of professionalism, value neutrality and objectivity. From our perspective, not only must media production courses play an important role within broader inquiry, they are particularly appropriate sites for the introduction of concepts such as representation and ideology, concepts fundamental to a more complete and satisfying understanding of the media as a cultural form.

However, to bring these concepts into an introductory video production course strains against the traditional canon of television production and, in doing so, can frustrate student expectations regarding the role of the class in relation to the greater structure of the department and academic major. This frustration can be rechanneled and transformed through the medium of pedagogy into the self-transformation of consciousness in which the student shifts from the passive *object* of instruction (that which is acted upon) into an active *subject* capable of acting upon and transforming the world. While we borrow from Freire this notion of transformation, there are obvious and significant differences between the populations in which these concepts are applied. In the system of higher education in the United States the role of *object* is often quite comfortable and secure. When critical pedagogical concepts are practiced in isolation (i.e., in a student's 1:00 class, but not in her 3:00) they can take on a character of random intellectual terrorist attacks. We cannot overemphasize the necessity for pedagogical restructuring throughout the entire curriculum, and the corresponding need for a renewed understanding of the role of the university itself in contemporary life.

"Crisis" Management

Organized disruptions of the established canon of television production represents a moment of crisis for both production teacher and production student. To recognize the established conventions of television production as undertheorized and acritical, and established models of production pedagogy as inadequate, creates a crisis in instructional (institutional) authority. In addressing such a crisis, the critical educator must avoid a return to familiar patterns of teaching versus research in which roles are changed from teacher (concerned with the reproduction of knowledge) to theorist/researcher (concerned with the production of knowledge)—and this is a difficult reaction to resist. After years of enculturation as an academic (college, graduate school, faculty appointments) this movement from lectern to library is almost a reflex action. However, in this movement, the flames of our schizophrenia are rekindled; this response reinforces the separation of theory from practice, itself mirrored in the traditional (and equally problematic) division between research and teaching. More important, such a response is a refusal to take pedagogy seriously. The bridge we hope to build between media studies (both its theory and practice) and critical pedagogy can work to disrupt this dichotomy of teaching versus research. Through the displacement of a transmission model of media training (or, the teaching of media reproduction), the teaching of media production is recast as an ongoing process involving the transformation of consciousness (and reformations of self) that takes place in the interaction among three agencies: the teacher, the learner and the knowledge that they together produce.

Critical studies (and everything that phrase in some way contains—structuralism, poststructuralism, feminism, postmodernism, subaltern studies, etc.) as they have been applied to analyses of contemporary entertainment media, have redirected attention toward questioning the ways in which the popular media represent the world and its various relations. The focus these projects have shared has been in these efforts directed at defamiliarization, demystification and denaturalization, that is, the critical project of deconstructing the cultural mechanisms of hegemony that support a dominant ideology. In the system of higher education in the United States, this project has had only very limited success in moving beyond the confines of the graduate classroom, doctoral dissertation, professional meeting and academic journal, into the broader public sphere. Critical pedagogy, however, in its disruption of the distancing dichotomy of teacher and scholar, and in its repositioning of teacher and learner within a historically resituated academic discourse, represents the added affirmative goals of a project of reconstruction. In the disruption (and reconstruction) of the traditional distinctions between theory and practice, a critical pedagogy of the media classroom offers a pedagogy of hope in the collapse of new theory into new practice. It is in this manner in particular that the union of critical pedagogy and television production can offer the real promise of the feedback of theory in practice.

The force with which the dichotomy of theory/practice has attached itself to media production curricula has worked to impede critical inquiry into the greater social and political implications of television production. While much of our effort is directed at developing the critical media literacy skills of our students, reading the media represents only one facet of this process. The media production classroom (television in particular) offers an added dimension of writing the media, the missing piece of the literacy process.

(Critical) Production Equipment

Having taught both introductory and advanced video production classes at various universities throughout the past decade, we believe that the introductory video production course is best taught in a single-camera field production context. This is in contrast to the multiple-camera studio environment that dominates introductory classes at most institutions.[2] The studio environment encourages an acritical focus upon mainstream entertainment styles and techniques. Each piece of equipment is introduced, each crew position is explained. Instructors, needing production models in which to rotate students through the equipment and positions, inevitably call upon *news*, *talk*, *sports* and related models. By the time the exercises are complete, the class is either over or almost over, and the techniques and conventions of mainstream entertainment television have been ingrained as the norm to which all other approaches must be contrasted and compared. In this approach there is little time to question the assumptions that underlie these conventions.

In a single-camera EFP (electronic field production) approach, each student is asked to consider from the start the ethical and political implications of message design. Along with basic instruction in camera movement, shot composition and selection, sound recording, lighting, and so on, each student must also examine issues of representation and the construction of meaning. Single-camera video coupled with cuts-only editing instruction employs the model of the documentary for its basic introductory instruction. Documentary allows for (even encourages) a combination of seminar/readings sessions with workshops in video production—all in the same course. The practice and theory of television production can be centered around an introduction to a set of key concepts. While beginning class sessions introduce the camera, lighting, and sound recording equipment, these are relatively straightforward and easy to operate, and require relatively small investments of class time. Allowing students to go out and shoot footage and return and begin to manipulate it in an edit bay (both individually and in small groups) opens up spaces in introductory lecture/discussions for closer considerations of the various epistemological assumptions that underlie the conventions of video production. These spaces also allow for an open discussion of media education as a value-loaded academic and social discourse. Questioning these assumptions offers each student the opportunity to bring into the discussion his or her own history of experience as, among other things, a *media major.*

Student production exercises in a single-camera approach allow students to begin to find a voice within the clutter of equipment and program styles.

Individual student projects that focus on biography, family history or urban history develop students as message creators while students in a studio context are still struggling with individual pieces of production equipment in isolation (e.g., learning how to produce an electronic key or matte effect on the video switcher without understanding the role of that effect in the greater and more complex context of message design). When students are challenged and can feel themselves developing as message creators, class discussions can become more deeply involved in the theory that informs this new practice.

Contemporary media theory works to defamiliarize dominant modes of representation. Critical pedagogy works to defamiliarize dominant modes of instructional practice. Throughout both of these processes new vocabularies are required as new territories of knowledge open up. In the teaching of (media) theory and criticism it is the language of contemporary critical discourse that creates the greatest initial resistance on the part of students (this is particularly true of undergraduates). One important element in the early weeks of instruction is building a critical conceptualization of language, not as a value-free neutral vehicle for the expression of "objective" thought, but as interwoven with the preexistent values in which it is historically and culturally situated.

Single-camera video production, far better than its studio counterpart, can be connected to film studies in readings and discussions. Excursions into film history (and a literature of greater depth than television history) can encourage consideration of history and historical understanding, a discussion that can be drawn across media into the economic and political history of broadcasting and into an ideological analysis of contemporary media practice. While there are obvious limitations on such discussions in the context of an introductory production class, further links can be drawn between these peripheral discussions and other classes in broadcast history (within the department) and social history (outside the department). Critical pedagogy insists upon the decompartmentalization of knowledge (the compartmentalization of which has been a central project of the modern university), the setting free of the genie of historical consciousness. As Gregory Kealey argues:

Historical understanding teaches us to transform the seemingly fixed and internal in our lives into things that can be changed. It teaches . . . people that the structures surrounding them have been made and remade over and over. It teaches that we live in history. (quoted in Giroux, 1988, 3)

This approach allows a production teacher to integrate elements from both film and television in discussions of history, technology, economics and theory. As students are asked to scrape away and examine the complex structures beneath the individual shot or narrative sequence, distinctions between theory and practice begin to erode. It is in this erosion that we might begin to understand better the particular appropriateness of the introductory production classroom as a site for the application of critical pedagogy. In the context of the single-camera approach to video production, the use of the documentary form in production projects also seems particularly appropriate in light of pedagogy's insistence upon the power and necessity of the student's voice in the production of knowledge. Relevant here is documentary theorist Bill Nichols's insistence upon the filmmaker's voice in the production of the documentary:

Far too many contemporary filmmakers appear to have lost their voice. Politically, they forfeit their own voice for that of others (usually characters recruited to the film and interviewed). Formally, they disavow the complexities of voice, and discourse, for the apparent simplicities of an unquestioned empiricism (the world and its truths exist; they need only be dusted off and reported). . . . We may think we hear history or reality speaking to us through a film, but what we actually hear is the voice of the text, even when that voice tries to efface itself. (1983, 19)

A critical pedagogy of media production must address the ethical and moral dimensions of the structures and processes of media production-as-practice, dimensions ignored in more traditional approaches to media production training. While recent media and cultural theory has focused upon the assumptions underlying the production and reception of entertainment film and television, this theoretical work has, for various reasons, failed to impact upon the curricular mission of undergraduate radio-television degree programs. This failure has two results: first, it heightens the inherently schizophrenic character of production/research faculty positions; second, it furthers the degree to which undergraduate media degree programs are ethically and morally complicit in their roles in the reproduction and maintenance of dominant cultural values. The proposed bridging of the literatures of critical pedagogy and media studies offers potential solutions to both problems.

NOTES

1. For example, these tensions are present in the labeling of some professional meetings, academic journals and other outlets for research as exclusively "critical" or "mainstream."

2. The choice between studio facilities and small-format field/edit facilities is not simply a conceptual one. It is, in fact, also a matter of efficiency in time and money spent in the education of our students. A typical studio, equipped with multicamera setups, complex switcher, Chyron, DVE, and so on, limits the amount of time each student can actually practice with and use the equipment. For example, a typical facility will have invested the bulk of its money in one or two studios and perhaps a remote van. A much smaller portion is allotted to field equipment. In cost-benefit terms, the typical investment is around $6,000 per student for multicam productions, and only about $1,000 per student for field uses. But what is startling is that approximately 50 students per year are served by the multicam facilities, whereas over 300 students are served by the field/edit equipment. In a typical department an equivalent investment in field equipment versus studio will yield up to 10 times as much student access per dollar spent.

Chapter Seven

Building Bridges

The university remains a site of cultural struggle, an arena of cultural politics. Its diminished role in the public sphere serves to emphasize the urgent need for the reclarification, redefinition and reestablishment of what is fundamentally a moral and ethical mission. It is in the confusing transformative culture of the late twentieth century (confusion and transformation marked by economic crisis, political upheaval, restructuring of world markets and a general postmodern melancholia) that we locate the importance of media studies—in the need for a critical understanding of media power, and in confronting the role of the university in training students for media industries. A critical theory of media education offers a pedagogy of empowerment, resistance, invention and hope. The building of bridges between critical pedagogy and media studies represents a first step in this project.

This book is about critical pedagogy's contribution to a project of critique and reformation of mass communication/media studies as it is, in general, currently represented by departments and curricula within United States universities and colleges. Our arguments throughout the preceding chapters are built upon a foundation of a critical theory of the media. The mass media, within the impenetrably dense and complex structures in which it presents an unceasing flow of news and entertainment programming, represent the single most powerful and concentrated source for the transmission, reproduction and maintenance of dominant culture. The majority of bachelor degree programs in media exist simply to train the next generation of docile media employees who, as young malleable laborers, enter the industry and contribute to the reproduction of its continued existence. It is within these conditions that our lives as critics/scholars/teachers are stamped with the temper of schizophrenia.

The confusion of character that fans the flames of media studies' schizophrenia can only be understood against the backdrop of mass communication's emergence within the greater historical context of the changing character of the modern university and the ongoing struggle over the goals of public education in the United States. And it is in a critical theory of media education that we have gone looking for a possible way out of the tangled schizophrenia of (media) theory torn asunder from (media) practice.

What must emerge eventually as a framing structure is a critical sociology of media education examining the various links between media curriculum and the media marketplace. The mass media play a principal role in disseminating the images and ideas that shape contemporary life. What is crucial is that our students understand how the media are historically situated and how political, economic, social and cultural decisions have led to the type of media we now have both in this country and around the world. In light of the media's ubiquity, this knowledge is vital in recognizing the enormous cultural power of media institutions to define what constitutes knowledge: the power to certify reality as reality. What is crucial is that children and adolescents begin to gain exposure to these concepts (to the simple idea that television might be less "real" than it may at first appear) in primary and secondary schooling as an integral part of developmental curricula, and at home in the context of discussion and exposure to alternative media forms. What is crucial is that this knowledge inflect each student's decision to major in media studies/mass communication. What is crucial is that this knowledge inform in a basic and fundamental manner university curricula, and the university's relationship to media industries.

PRELIMINARY PEDAGOGICAL CONSIDERATIONS

The University's Place in the Transformation of the Public Sphere

In many ways the modern university has replaced its function as a creative/subversive institution[1] with a fondness for structure and organization among its parts, and the rigid compartmentalization of knowledge within these structures. Whether this represents a character flaw of modernism in general, or the more recent result of economic insecurity (or both), the resulting orientation toward regimentation and professionalism has established borders within which most departments and programs of mass communication operate. Our efforts here have been directed at the redefinition of one small piece of a much larger picture, that is, the modern university. We are tightly constrained by the necessarily limited scope of our own efforts (individually, collectively, in our writing and in our teaching) and by our melancholy over thoughts of a future in which even the smallest success seems uncertain.

However (and melancholy demands a "however" to prevent a descent into full-blown depression), the energy released from a fuller, more complete theorization of pedagogy radiates far beyond the confines of the media production classroom or the media studies department, outward through the university's structure as a whole, even within the greater structures of its relations to the world at large. This project requires all of our combined efforts and talents and, while goal-driven to an extent, has no real end to it. This is a project of redefinition. The question that rests beneath the surface of what we do here asks about connecting our work as individuals to this greater project.

In the midst of complexities, assumptions, questions and confusions too many to number, we struggle with a project of redefinition. Our hope is to restore some coherency to the project of furthering an understanding of the role of education in democratic development. In this project, democracy is always understood as both process and, by definition, incomplete, perpetually unfinished. From this perspective, schools are seen as sites of democratic, public sphere activity, as institutions whose focus is not singularly upon the training of contented labor for industry.

We have seen that the compartmentalizing character of modern living works so effectively to keep the status quo propped up (regardless of its banality) simply because it prevents the various compartments of our lives from connecting. This fragmented existence must be challenged from the perspective of a utopian alternative. Writing about literacy, Paulo Freire describes an "authentic" existence, a process of becoming human in which a more complete humanity is achieved through the growth of a critical awareness of one's material conditions (political, economic, cultural, etc.) There is, we believe, a fuller humanity, a more authentic existence than the one we (most of us) live here on the edges of the twentieth century. The action necessary to enter this "other" future is a function of reconnecting the many facets of our lives. Education in general, and the university in particular, are essential pieces in this process. "Go to college and become more human" must somehow, in effect, replace the guidance counselor's emphasis upon a bachelor's degree and a better job.

This project of reconnection necessitates pedagogy's extension beyond the walls of the classroom and the university. This extension enables a diversity of voices to add their concerns to the agenda of the common good.

A curriculum (and university) transformed in such a manner is capable of the vigorous critical praxis necessary to reinvigorate public debate in passionate discourse. One way pedagogy will extend beyond the classroom and campus is through educators searching out connections to others engaged in social and political struggles in order to open up new spaces that provide new opportunities to rebuild and renew our understanding and experience of democracy. Pedagogy insists upon this expansion, upon these connections; this understanding of pedagogy insists upon the building of bridges connecting us to a fuller existence as human beings.

As people we still stumble along (if not in darkness then in very poor light), looking for the perfect point in the circle to begin: The problems with education are the result of problems with social formations, which must be addressed by changes in education, which cannot be made without first making changes in social relations, which are reproduced by an educational system, which must be changed, but cannot without first changing the social, political and economic base upon which it operates, but changes in those structures must be preceded by more fundamental changes in cultural relations, which can only be effected through organized educational efforts, which cannot be undertaken without first addressing problematic relations among social formations, which effectively cripple efforts to change educational systems, and so on.

Our confusion and inaction results from an illusion that we exist somehow separate and apart from this circle, that we are somewhere else watching it turn from a distance and waiting for the beginning to come round again. We are, of course, part of it, inside and turning with it, caught up in its motion. Pedagogy's hardest lesson (the point where theory and practice collapse upon each other and action can begin) is simply that we must begin to act wherever and from whatever position we find ourselves.

As academics/media educators we are active players in the various relationships between our departments and universities, and an array of public and private institutions. We can take action in rethinking existing policies: those that connect our classrooms to mainstream broadcast industries rather than forms of alternative media, those that vocationalize and instrumentalize our curricula, those that relegate us to secondary units in support of university public relations. Our actions, individually and collectively, must be firmly grounded in the (re)commitment to the university as public sphere and to the (re)definition of education in the context of the humane values of democracy and social responsibility. Active instruction in the participatory character of democracy, and the various bases of the choices that underpin this participation, becomes the most basic ("bottom-line") function of education within a democracy.[2]

Integrating the Cultural and Political with Practice

The big question is, of course: How do we connect our work as individuals to this greater project? How do we build these bridges from the specifics of our curriculum to the world beyond the classroom and library? In a critical pedagogy of media education, the realm of media practice, that is, the traditional areas of media management, production, planning and writing, would be interwoven with the critical analysis of media institutions and practices. Rather than encouraging and reinforcing feelings of schizophrenia, such an integration would allow us to bring to bear a pedagogy of cultural politics onto those very sites of media education (Introduction to Television Production, Broadcast Management, Introduction to Message Design, etc.) that are most often left to professional/apolitical approaches. As shown in the previous chapter, this kind of curricular integration actively avoids the sterility of media critique disconnected from media practice. Central to this integration, and particularly appropriate in a media studies curriculum, the use of contemporary popular culture texts (e.g., music, film and television) offers a means of bridging the distance between student experience and critical work—a means of exploring media forms in depth while opening up space for students' creative expression.

Looking at the current state of undergraduate media education in the United States, refracted through the lens of critical pedagogy, we find in place structures that silence a pedagogy of cultural politics, and undermine the goals of liberal education in a democratic society. A credo of professionalism divides and separates students' lives into roles of producer and consumer. The student in the classroom assumes the role of audience member, passively awaiting the unthreatening arrival of his or her education, while continually irritated by the inability to change channels. It is the central challenge for a reworked media curriculum to turn the media back upon itself, to activate and combine student intellect and creativity in a project of critique and reflection. This is what the sum of the parts of undergraduate education in general must become if we (students, faculty, everybody) are to put our lives in order.

This disruption of the traditional media classroom is certainly not without its own set of special problems. Beginning television production courses are often the territory of junior faculty, who must navigate the complex (and often unmapped) paths toward tenure and promotion. For critical media pedagogy to disrupt the expectations of media students is one thing; for junior media faculty to disrupt those expectations is another thing again in the broader context of professional academic life. We believe that the problematic (schizophrenic) character of teaching media is heightened in the specific context of teaching production. Production courses become both schizophrenic and ironic. The schizophrenia is enhanced by the conceptualization of a professionalism openly hostile to critical reflection; the irony is that the media production classroom ought to represent among the more ideal settings for the creative discussion of media culture and cultural politics. In doing this, however, we also shift the emphasis away from the passive transmission of "objective" information (the "answers" to questions on "objective" tests) to the active search for better questions.

Another challenge to pedagogy is in addressing the insecurity that this shift in emphasis engenders. Insecurity is the natural state of anyone seeking wisdom. Insecurity is also highly threatening to undergraduate students, who have been enculturated since grade school in an educational system in which the active participation of students is most often viewed as disruptive behavior. Within such a system, feelings of insecurity are considered unnatural. The ("natural") emphasis upon individual competition and the equation of academic success with grade point average represents an unspoken ideology of education. In the service of ideology, hegemony naturalizes and transforms the arbitrary, historical and political into normative "common sense," unquestioned understanding of cultural relations. Critical media pedagogy calls for a corresponding restructuring of this basic character of university schooling and new definitions of (in particular) success and failure. It calls for a new role for insecurity in the active pursuit of knowledge by students who are active participants in their own educations, their individual growth as democratic citizens, their entry into a fuller humanity.

Rethinking the Classroom

We must confront the fact that virtually all media pedagogy within undergraduate education in the United States operates within a set of seemingly intractable constraints. The cumulative character of these constraints (those of the credit hour, structure of major, career option, job tracks, etc.) results in the continual separation of theory and practice, the reproduction of extant media culture and the formation of our schizophrenia. As we argued earlier, the key to the redefinition of the relation of work and culture in both the university and society at large is in understanding work as the force that builds a democratic society rather than simply one part in a system of economic markets. This project of redefinition and rethinking the basic components of what we now think of as education may be more possible at this moment than it has been in decades.

The economic turmoil of recent years has had a profound impact upon colleges and universities: faculty positions have been eliminated, teaching loads increased, class sizes enlarged, benefits cut back and in some cases entire programs, and even departments, have been abandoned. Universities have scrambled to find new models, borrowed mostly from business, for fiscal management and have tried various new approaches to the management of resources and personnel.

One result of this upheaval is that the university has entered a period of experimentation. The percentage of returning adult students continues to rise and efforts to recruit and accommodate these students also increase. More and more, administrators are turning to new communication technologies as a creative means of addressing economic difficulties. New combinations of technologies (telephone, computer and videotape in particular) are being employed in the new arena of "distance learning." Increasingly, perhaps unintentional coalition of critical educators and administrators is at the forefront of those calling for the rethinking of traditional educational concepts like the classroom, credit hour, major, and so on. The residential college offering a four-year degree program to a population of 18- to 22-year-old students is fading into our past as the population shifts in irreversible ways. The urban university in particular, with open admissions and commitment to minority recruitment, has emerged as a site for the redefinition of university education in the next century.

This project of redefinition either will be accomplished entirely by university administrators with emphasis upon fiscal realities and increasing competition for education dollars, or will be a project in which critical educators can take an active role in the planning and design of new curricular models that both open new territories within the university and explore new connections between the university and the community, creating new sites for student creativity/work/practice and the potential for social and democratic renewal.

In the specific context of media studies, traditional career-defined majors will disappear, in part, as budget priorities and economic shortfalls force universities to make cuts. Departments of radio/television/film usually enroll large numbers of majors. Those programs with a strict industry focus, however, are among the most expensive on a per-student basis due to the tremendous expense of media production facilities and equipment. Current economic realities (and virtually all projections for the future) provide an extensive body of evidence for critical media educators hoping to convince administrators to shift emphasis away from professional job training for mainstream industries also feeling the full effect of economic turmoil and overcrowded with entry-level personnel. Instead, we believe that the shift to a broader based liberal arts curriculum with an emphasis upon critical thinking can be more attractive to the changing student population, and also attractive to an increasing number of university administrators.

The overall goal of a new media curriculum is joined with that of the liberal arts in a transformation of the public sphere. The emergence of a new media studies curriculum must correspond with similar transformations across the university. These transformations will be led by creative new reconceptualizations of the traditional elements of undergraduate education: the idea of the four-year bachelor's degree (already antiquated) will vanish as the normal way to go to college; the idea of the classroom as it has existed since the beginnings of education will be expanded to include communities of students spread out across different locations, accessing course content at different times, sometimes individually and sometimes collectively; the semester system comprised of fifteen weeks and blocks of three-credit hour courses meeting regularly throughout the week will be open to challenge and change; most important perhaps, the elimination of the traditional classroom will open many new spaces for the forging of new connections and coalitions between university and community, shaking the foundations of that dichotomy and the related dichotomies of student/citizen and ivory tower/real world.

The phenomenon of the convergence of various communication technologies will be a driving force behind many of these transformations. These new technologies and their application represent a new territory across which many future struggles will be played out. Economic difficulties have created, in their wake, the possibility for the redefinitions important to the project of critical pedagogy. Critical educators must be prepared to take full advantage of what these technologies represent. New technologies always have the potential to widen the already pronounced gaps between those without the necessary resources. These technologies also have the potential to democratize the information resources they represent. This democratizing potential requires the active role of critical educators in the application of these technologies, and in the design of the new systems and structures that will redefine the role of the university in the next century.

Again, media studies is a particularly appropriate location from which to pursue such an involvement. Technology and the media have long been synonymous, and the lure of new technologies has long been a major attraction to undergraduates. From our perspective, each communications technology represents another site for the exploration of the core set of fundamental questions: How does media create meaning? What is the special nature of mediated reality? What is the role of this technology in society? What does it do to further or retard the progress of democracy?

What are the ethical concerns for the media practitioner in this area? How is this technology historically situated? Continually asking these questions in the context of media practice offers a means toward the reunification of theory with practice.

THE OVERARCHING GOALS OF THE MEDIA STUDIES CURRICULUM

Rethinking the nature of the department and the classroom precludes taking a "cookbook" approach to recasting the media studies curriculum. The great variety of institutional settings, the particularities of geography and the varieties of undergraduate and faculty composition further preclude us from offering a monolithic curricular revision suitable for all situations. Neither can we predict how the university will shift in the near future, as it responds to the conditions we have outlined above. However, we can offer a number of tools for refashioning the media studies curriculum, as well as examples that illustrate their use.

In conceptualizing the overall curriculum for a media studies program, faculty should bear in mind a number of overarching principles and conditions of education as characterized by a critical pedagogy. First, the curriculum must develop in dialogue with the concerns of students. This is not a matter of simply adapting to predefined career needs, but means attending to conscious and unconscious critical thoughts and feelings that surface in students' everyday lives. Second, a narrow vocationalism should be rejected, which means absolutely no job tracks. Third, theory and practice must be integrated in all classwork and outside experiences. In addition, the curriculum's coherency should be based in the principles of critical pedagogy; that is, whatever form the curriculum takes, its individual components should cohere around the fundamental concerns of transforming the public sphere and developing students' capacities as citizens (who happen to see the media as a potential site of work). Fourth, no particular classroom arrangements—past enrollment models, job track mechanisms, cattle-call "weed-out" courses, time-bound structures (e.g., seminars or workshops only in senior year)—should dictate the structure of the curriculum. Fifth, forms of popular culture that impact students' lives should be given primary focus, without artificially separating high from low culture. Sixth, the curriculum should address pedagogy itself; that is, a moment of self-reflection on the issues that have formed the center of this book should be openly debated and worked on.

Bearing in mind these principles, the student's degree program can now be unified throughout the curriculum. Classes in the major area now connect in various ways with classes from other required areas throughout the school. Central to this unification is the overarching goal of the development of a *critical media literacy*. Within the broader context of liberal education, the project we label as critical media literacy has been designated as critical thinking, a complex concept that extends far beyond the simple notion of sharpened cognitive skills. Developing a critical literacy and thinking critically in the context of a liberal education suggest the development of skills that extend into the public sphere, public discourse and join in an effort for the public good.

In the context of a liberal arts education and media studies, we have identified a set of ten goals associated with these skills:[3] (1) critical use of written languages in both analysis and production of media; (2) the conceptual understanding of empirical methods and the informed use of mathematical tools; (3) knowledge of the conceptual frameworks deployed by the media and by attempts to study the media, that is, the manner in which ways of knowing are conditioned by class, racial identity, ethnicity, institutional traditions, gender, philosophic perspectives and political objectives; (4) understanding science and technology in perspective, particularly the manner in which human forms of knowing and feeling are transformed and/or developed through the media's use of these advanced technologies; (5) understanding the present as a historical situation and seeing history as the ever-present context of the formation of media structures and content; (6) sensitivity to the various roles of art and artists in culture; (7) understanding the process of creativity, discovery and problem solving; (8) knowledge of other cultures and a strong sense of the world's cultural pluralism, particularly in the forms of media production, distribution and consumption; (9) understanding the complex ethical dimensions of media professional behavior and the ethical contexts of knowledge; and (10) understanding the formation of media public policy, and seeking commitments to social and political justice.

Media Pedagogy as Media Literacy

The overarching principles and conditions of critical pedagogy and the areas of critical literacy discussed above are not intended as a blueprint for media studies programs. Other areas of knowledge and activity can and should be developed. In what follows, the direction for media studies that we propose, as much as possible, stresses the current context of program development and attempts to point out a direction that might actually develop given the current constraints. Ultimately, we hope for a future in which media studies reunites the students' and faculty's roles as producers, critics and consumers of media. These roles are united in that together they can be taken as indicative of an overall conception of our functions as citizens. In this context, we begin to see that a critical media pedagogy is primarily a project of media literacy, broadly conceived.

This project of literacy must begin within the concrete "knowledges" that are required if we are educating students into taking up a serious concern with citizenship. It has long struck us as odd that the vast majority of students leave school from age 16 on with extremely hazy levels of knowledge about matters that will concern them most in their lives. We are referring to their knowledge of: (1) personal health, nutrition and medical matters; (2) social and sexual interaction between individuals and groups; (3) the structure and operation of the state, political organizations, local government, welfare benefits, housing, and so on—in short, the economic and institutional underpinning of society (Alvarado, 1990, 2).

Currently, however, the popular media works more toward the erasure of these knowledge forms, and in support of the regressive postmodern definition of freedom as a broad choice of consumption objects. The contemporary popular media fragments, creates dissensus, threatens/erases the practical base of knowledge that marginal or powerless groups need in order to take hold of their everyday lives and work toward changing their historical conditions. Here we are up against the other "practical" education that students need and desire. Here, critical media pedagogy for the undergraduate school dovetails with the broader project of developing a critical media literacy in society at large. We propose that this media literacy dimension of media studies is the added element necessary to integrate fully the curriculum.

Any attempt to define the goals of the curriculum must attend to the multiple roles of the student in their interaction with media as career choice, as area of intellectual inquiry and as source of information and pleasure. The dominant model of defining the curricular goals of media study stresses the producer role of the student; here we bring in those other roles—critic, and consumer/audience member—that complete the picture of student as citizen.

Given the existing social formation, the modes of communication are operated primarily in the interests of oppression. This is not a simple mechanical operation, but is tied to the hegemonic conjuncture of market, military and political interests. However, this operation of the media is not a seamless operation closing off all possibilities of alternative use. The media is a leaky system that is struggled over in its production and reception. We can conceive of media literacy as a process of developing a counter-hegemonic project. We propose that media literacy develop a three-pronged attack: first, a practice of re-reading the media; second, a practice of affective reflexivity—a remapping of subject positions; and third, a practice of rewriting or developing vital strategies of authorship. These practices further the goals of critical thinking that we have outlined above and fit within and across the 10 categories laid out there. This model of media literacy serves to reduce the rather unwieldy enumeration of principles and goals to a three-pronged attack that allows the direction of the curriculum to be conceptualized in a more clear and concise manner.

Re-Reading the Media

Contemporary media are themselves pedagogical in function; they contribute to constructions of knowledge and the subject of knowledge. Thus, a first step in a critical media literacy program involves the practice of ideology critique in a confrontation with the text. In the context of postmodernism, this means educating students to become media literate in a world of changing representations. This entails reworking the traditional practice of ideology critique, which tends to locate meaning in the text as an isolated object of interpretation. Instead, the practice of critique must involve a number of considerations: (1) the critical reading of how cultural texts are regulated by various discursive codes; (2) how such texts express and represent different ideological interests; (3) how they might be taken up differently by various subjects in different contexts.

In this process of literacy acquisition, ideological criticism is an important first stage in the initial task of taking apart or breaking down the "natural" and "eternal," and its replacement with the cultural and the historical. It is here also where hegemony as the mechanism of ideology is introduced. It is in this introduction to media hegemony that a full array of rupturing practices, processes of demythologizing and denaturalizing—that is, the processes of making the invisible visible—are undertaken. And it is here also where the contributions of contemporary structuralist and post-structuralist literary theory can be examined through the power of its critique in the disintegration of the traditional source-centered transmission models of mass communication. And it is here where we might begin to consider critical pedagogy's corresponding disruption of transmission models of education, and to examine the collapse of the distancing dichotomies of (among others) reader/writer and teacher/student, which is necessary for the potential of both media and media education to be realized.

Media as a pedagogical machine is not simply a producer of meanings (an encoding of truths to be appropriated by the minds of the audience); it also produces "subjectivity." Students need to engage media representations as constructive of meanings that discursively set the boundaries of how reality may be approached. They need also to look at how these meanings are mobilized in everyday life, how they hook up with emotional (affective) commitments that are historically situated.

At the level of critique the project of media literacy is to break down this practice by reconstituting the context of media communication and the material identity and agency of the reader/writer. Ideology critique is not disconnected from institutional, legal, cultural, political and economic factors. The contexts of the text are crucial both to the reading of its historical construction and as the gateway to the further questions: Who produces images? For whose consumption? For what purposes? What alternative images are thereby excluded?

Further, we stress that the media must be "deconstructed where it hurts," that is, we need to connect this critique to everyday life and those areas of student experience to which they are actively committed. Ideology critique is counterproductive at best when it simply draws upon an academic jargon to find various myths. Instead, we must question naturalized knowledge, pinpoint areas of ideology that students connect to and that make a difference in their lives. We must take seriously the experiences through which students constitute their identities and draw upon them as means for criticizing the dominant culture (Giroux, 1988, 175). This leads us to consider the second area of counterhegemonic practice in critical media literacy.

Affective Reflexivity: Remapping Subject Positions

Denaturalizing the text is not an isolated practice. If we know and can see that MTV is sexist in its representation, what implications follow? Do we then still watch MTV? The idea is not to batter and condemn popular forms (the lesson is not, "OK, now don't watch television"). Instead, we must attend to the affective investments that students bring to the text—why do they watch what they watch, who do they watch it with and what do they do with it?

Critical media literacy must offer a practice of dialogue with students in order that commitments, styles of consumption and investments in the media be foregrounded, questioned and understood. Students must question the text and what they do with the text. Teachers must take seriously students' commitments to and affective investments in various forms of popular culture in order both to interrogate critically self-production and to draw out student activity that opens up possibilities for counterhegemonic practices. Media literacy must draw out these responses in the context of the historically bounded meanings available in media production, the interpretive assets available to the reader and the reading formations that readers bring to acts of reception. This literacy of reading and rewriting involves asking "Who I am when I see this?" In asking students to examine their multiple subjectivity in relation to media constructions, media literacy must turn the focus back onto the specificity of subject positions generated in media reading.

Finally, being media literate means both having a voice, and giving the other a voice—seeing one's subjectivity in the threat of the other and then overcoming that threat in the recognition of the partiality of one's own perspective. Media literacy is not a practice that takes place in isolation. In order to understand the media, one's self, one's relation to it, one must be able to speak (with a voice) and be able to recognize who is speaking in the media and who is not speaking. By recognizing the other, the difference that exists in a positive sense, we break down the dichotomies that structure capitalist hegemony—core/periphery, majority/minority, first world/third world, and so on. Knowledge must be reinvented and reconstructed by inviting students to be border crossers (Giroux, 1990, 124). Such a pedagogy defines itself as a project of educating students to take the stand of the other, to practice an analysis of their own conditions and to believe that they can make a difference.

Rewriting and the Vital Strategy of Authorship

Finally, a critical media literacy produces a transformative alternative practice. A mode of problematizing, this course of action produces, "against the grain," an alternative attack and creation of representation. Students need to be encouraged to invent counterrepresentations and counterforms of organization and evaluation. First of all, active reading should itself be seen as a form of production, a form of countermemory that produces a reinscription that counters our present forms of truth and justice.

Add to this an active writing—an alternative practice—a direct handling of the tools and processes of media practice. In this way the concepts of reader/writer within the emergence of a critical media literacy are connected to notions of audience and producer. To return to our initial paradox: given the technologies available and their potential for the democratization of the media, how can the oppositional potential of these media be so easily thwarted? Further, and more specific to our purposes here, how can these new technologies be used in the creation of a counterhegemony in support of the long revolution?

Both television (or, in its expanded sense, video) and the classroom possess a potential to represent two democratic public spheres. As such, they also represent two crucial sites in the formation of subjectivities. Access to both (by access we refer to all levels of operations, programming and ownership) are fundamental aspects of the ongoing struggle over the sociocultural status quo, and all that it entails. Both the classroom and the contemporary entertainment and news media are sites of struggle over the creation, recreation and maintenance of our individual understanding of the values and relations that arise from our collective understanding of past, present and future—the way things are and the way things could be—and struggles over the celebration of difference and voices critical of the way things are, or their continued exclusion and suppression.

TOOL KIT FOR THE MEDIA STUDIES CURRICULUM

The project of critical media literacy provides the overarching goals of a transformed media curriculum. The three counterhegemonic practices are not separate areas under which specific courses would be grouped, rather all courses should incorporate elements of all of these practices. It is now time to offer some suggestions as to how this project can be implemented in a concrete program of media study. We need to consider how the goals of media literacy can be taken up in transforming the media studies curriculum: how will students define their program of study, what new shape will the common core curriculum for media studies now take, under what domains can courses be grouped that allow for both a centrality to media literacy's three areas and a coherent attention to specific content areas of media study?

Defining Student Curricular Goals

The dominant model for developing curricular goals relies upon the banking concept of schooling, in which job tracks, media-defined areas of information and current uses of technology lead to a constraining set of skill areas that further lead to rigid requirement structures. As a result, students place themselves within categories that are predefined by the department, and their interests are dictated by a year-by-year plan. Education becomes a matter of fulfilling requirements, and course selection is mandated by time constraints and credit accumulation. In the typical department, students complete a core of lecture courses in their freshman year, often set up simply to fulfill FTE (Full Time Employment) production, then proceed to define their entire college education based upon a one-time choice. They choose a set of courses defined by job areas (based on the scant information learned by rote in their introductory classes) and lock themselves into a set of specialized courses that promise (unsuccessfully) to give them the skills they need. A nonprofessional curriculum can just as easily fall into this pattern, setting goals in terms of critical tracks, defined by sequences in criticism, law, international communication, history, and so forth. This mode of defining curricular goals and structures still results in a rigid compartmentalized curriculum. A very typical situation is one in which departments are divided between "pro" students and "theory" students, who simply don't talk to each other.

We propose beginning with a very different model of goal setting, one that steers the student away from rigidly imposed definitions. Any curriculum begins with goals; ideally the goals of faculty (working under a critical pedagogy) and the goals of students match up through a process of give and take. However, the faculty must set some parameters for goal determination and then set up a curriculum that can fulfill these goals.

Assuming a curriculum that fulfills the six conditions noted above, and one that addresses the centrality of media literacy, students might conceive of their programs of study in the following manner. The activities of studying the media and doing it would be recast as no more separate than the activities of theory and practice. Students would define their individual programs not as job tracks, but on the basis of knowledge areas, conceptual skills and practical focus in a plan of study that would be regularly reviewed and updated. For example, a student might define the degree program in the following way: knowledge areas—media and family, media and value questions, media effects on practitioners, reality and objectivity; conceptual skills—writing, planning and aesthetic design; practical focus—documentary.

Such a design would allow students a wide flexibility in creating individualized programs that would lead them on their own to define their education as liberal education. At the same time students would be able to translate these skills into a wider range of professional settings than traditional preprofessional track systems allow for. Further, these goals allow the student to alter their program of study as their knowledge and skills grow.

Ideally, students would come to this conception of their program based upon an introduction to the field in their first year of study. This requires that the principles of critical pedagogy and media literacy be introduced to students in a manner that leads them to reflect critically on the goals they wish to pursue. Again, ideally, this would involve give and take between faculty advisors and students as the students work through their first year of study. This procedure requires that media studies programs develop some notion of a common core through which students acquire a common body of knowledge, but one that allows them the flexibility to develop their own conceptualization of their goals in media study.

The Common Core: Four Domains of Critical Media Pedagogy

The goals of critical media literacy should form the background of both student reflection upon their programs of study and the curricular specifics developed by faculty. Particularly, these goals reform the conception of a common core for all majors in media studies.[4] Within the vocational approach the core usually consists of "throw-away" courses that offer sweeping overviews of communication and media. After the core is out of the way, students proceed to their "real" programs, tracks such as broadcast performance, management, journalism, and so on. It is this kind of radically alienating detachment of theory and practice that we seek to overcome in seeking to develop a common core based in the general goals outlined above.

We will refrain from designating specific courses that treat the goals of the curriculum by compartmentalizing them. The common core should instead introduce the student to all of the theoretical and practical elements that we have outlined. The implementation of such a program is a bewildering prospect given the number and variety of preconditions and liberal education goals. This potentially debilitating starting place can be mitigated by further grouping the pedagogical goals within a manageable number of conceptual areas that the common core would at least begin to address. Given the call for coherence within a flexible critical pedagogical structure, the actual areas that the curriculum addresses might be structured in a variety of ways. One possible configuration would place the complex set of interacting goals within four domains: critical, analytic and methodological skills; historical knowledge; citizenship, law and ethics; and the theoretical underpinnings of practice. Each of these domains has implications for all three areas of media literacy—re-reading, reflexive affectivity and rewriting (we will note these convergences as we discuss each domain).

Designing a core of courses would not involve developing one course for each of these areas, particularly not by taking an existing course, such as media criticism, and designating it as the critical, analytic and methodological course. Such a procedure would develop strictures, separations and inflexibilities similar to current track-oriented pedagogy. Instead, the core must develop a set of three or four courses that integrate these four areas of critical skills and knowledge so that students develop the sensitivity to see their further program as involving an integration of all of these areas. The idea of a common core stresses not just a common base of information, but rather the development of (1) a view of pedagogy, (2) a stance of seeing oneself as existing within a common community of other students and (3) a reflexive view of one's program as an area of inquiry.

We can now outline briefly the four domains of a critical media pedagogy, keeping in mind that these domains are not all-inclusive or separable into discrete classes. Further, these domains are not simply an introductory matter that is over once the core is completed—they are ever-present throughout the program of study. The common core should be, after all, an immersion experience—students diving into the theoretical and practical elements that will form their education.

Critical, Analytic and Methodological Skills

These skills will be acquired throughout the student's curriculum. Applied to their major, students will acquire the ability to analyze media messages—their aesthetic, social and ideological meanings. Students will develop a knowledge of the codes employed within various formats and genres of production, and an understanding of the diversity of expression possible within mass communication media. As part of a media studies curriculum, students will gain an ability to conceptualize their communicative purposes in terms of manipulating key visual and aural symbolic variables. Students will be encouraged to develop an analytical understanding of the background of their own work—to know what they are trying to say, why they want to say it and what agendas may lie behind their decisions. We can see here that the media literacy practices of re-reading and rewriting are directly addressed.

These same skills are brought to the forefront in inquiries into the nature of media as social phenomena, in examinations of the public sphere and in research of the audience's use of the media (reflexive affectivity). These skills are not simply applied to career-related strategies, but to all possible viewpoints of the study of the media—as a career area, as an abstract theoretical domain, as a key area of everyday life.

Historical Knowledge

Students will gain a knowledge of how the media are historically situated and how political, economic, social and cultural struggles and decisions have led to the type of media that we now have both in this country and around the world. Contemporary U.S. culture is characterized in part by an ahistorical consciousness that both reflects and encourages the naturalization of a complex and particular ideological condition (re-reading). Students should understand how dominant American media exist within a wider international sphere and how different cultures' use of media varies in different historical situations. It is almost universal for liberal arts degrees to require a world history sequence. We encourage such requirements in that they help set the broader stage for the media-specific history we consider essential to the goals of a critical curriculum: general history of media; history of radio, television, film, sound recording as institutions; history of policy and law; history of technology; history of genres; comparative history (these specific histories are, again, not separable isolated areas). The historical dimension is also directly pertinent to students' roles as consumers and producers. Any practice of media production involves knowledge of the history of production practices, and any understanding of how we use the media involves understanding the historical context in which our subjectivity is formed.

Citizenship, Law and Ethics

Exposure to and active engagement in the discourse of ethics and responsibility are crucial goals in light of media's immense power. The goals of a liberal education are rooted in the desire to foster a true democracy—one characterized by self-reflection, critical thinking and active engagement in the pursuit of social justice. Students must be made aware of the determinants of media practice that may foster or hinder the creation of an open and pluralistic public sphere, and of the issues surrounding class, race, ethnicity, sexual orientation and gender.

A commitment to openness and respect for difference must be encouraged. There is no area more concrete within media education, for students, inside and outside the classroom, will be challenged to define their place within a set of ethical and political choices. These choices range from working with diverse others on practical projects (rewriting), to responding to the sometimes heinous omissions of the media on issues of race, gender and class (re-reading), to the day-to-day interactions (reflexive affectivity) with a variety of others (faculty and students) that characterize the college experience (and more generally the experience of media use). If the lessons of theorizing and practicing citizenship are not concretely dealt with, then education has truly lost any sense of mission within the process of developing democratic life.

Theoretical Underpinnings of Practice

As we have stressed throughout this book, theory and practice must be integrated. There is a pleasure and purpose to the pursuit of theory for its own stake, but when isolated from practice of any kind, theorizing becomes a sterile exercise. On the practical front, we need to bear in mind that a faculty's immersion in theory may be enough to keep them always focused on theory's practical effects (even when they become saturated in the high ground of contemporary theoretical discourse), but students are always beginning somewhere else—defined by their youth, personal experience and the particular situation of going to college. Thus, the pleasures of theoretical work have the best chance of actually making a difference for students when this work is connected with other sites of their engagement. It may seem unduly apologetic to focus on making theory fun, but the alternative is to relegate theory to the basement of serious pain that it now occupies in most communication students' lives.

Instead, theory must be brought to bear on all the other areas of a critical media pedagogy. In such a program students will deal with conceptual theories as a process, involving societal structures and culture, the media as institution and content, and the audiences influenced by and influencing mediated content and/or media technologies. This involves basic theories surrounding issues involving institutional links; social, political and economic determinants; psychological, social and political outcomes; and language and symbol construction. Each of these particularities of theory is then brought to bear on practical matters of production, history, viewership, citizenship and ethics (again, each practice of media literacy is clearly addressed).

In the course of this integration of theory with practice, the affective dimension must be brought to the forefront. That which is weighty must be seen as light—theory must be seen in the grain of the creatively chosen angle in a video comedy, in the feelings of pleasure engendered by changing even the smallest aspect of the media. One must be able to tell a joke about theory and in the next moment perceive its deadly serious import.

Common Core Courses

Without proposing the classes that would define this core, we can suggest some possibilities both for modifying existing courses and conceptualizing wholly new courses. First of all, we recommend dispensing with course titles such as Introduction to Mass Communication, Introduction to Media Production, and so on. The use of the term "introduction" both relegates these courses to secondary status (cattle-call courses) and sets the student up to conceive of the material as simplistic and easy (the real stuff comes later). Instead, we propose that courses such as Mass Communication and Society, Media Institutions and Practices, Popular Culture, Critical Writing for the Media, Mass Media Process and Effect, Media Advertising and Society and Mass Media and Politics can be remolded to function in the common core. Some of these courses retain a level of generality that allows a media literacy approach to be easily adapted, and allow a shifting back and forth between various domains. Other courses listed here focus in on more specific areas, piquing student interest in substantive areas such as advertising, writing or journalism. However, the more specific content of these courses can be approached through the domains of skills and knowledges laid out above.

An even more fruitful way of designing the core would be to start anew with completely experimental classes, such as Video Meaning-making (integrating production, criticism, history of genres, ethical concerns and theories of representation and reception), The Public Sphere (immediately introducing an overarching concern with democratic media), Media as Pedagogy, Media and Social/Political Justice and Media Struggles around the World. Such courses would offer a world of opportunities for introducing students to the goals, processes and skills of media literacy.

Putting Media Pedagogy into Practice: Some Suggestions and Examples

Reorganizing a media studies curriculum around these domains is a difficult task, particularly in conceptualizing the actual classes in which these skills and knowledge areas are developed. We need to answer some possible objections to our approach and further concretize the overall curriculum by offering specific suggestions and examples.

Much of what we offer here is taken from our own experiences as junior faculty in communication departments at a number of different types of institutions (from small private liberal arts colleges to large urban universities, with various stops between). Efforts to revise curricula with a broadcast/professional focus into a broader and more critically reflective model encounter a variety of obstacles. A common complaint is that a liberal arts curriculum is too generalist in nature; students are given a smattering of history, theory, and so on, but lack the depth to "do" anything. A program that had direct connections to the "real world" of broadcasting is being abandoned for one that has little connection to that "real world" of practice.

These objections are linked directly to the dichotomies we hope to disrupt, each traceable back to the initial separation of theory from practice (the "big bang" of dichotomies). In our efforts to cast off the structures that grew into place rooted in these dichotomies, we must begin at the beginning. We must avoid the reproduction of these same dichotomies in our curriculum. We must not separate theory and practice into separate classes ("boring" and "fun"). Rather, we must find new ways of folding the one into the other.

Another immediate objection is that in replacing neatly drawn "info" areas with a complex set of goals and domains, we are simply creating a situation of confusion for both students and faculty. "This semester, I have to teach/take Video Production I and Broadcast Journalism" is clear and concise for both faculty member and student. We rather flippantly respond, "Good, confusion and complexity are precisely what is needed!" We gladly give up the catalog of info approach, set course titles, clear tracks of study and neat areas of faculty expertise, for these are the mechanisms that have created media studies' most intractable problems. This being said, we can look at the traditional content of media studies and assess where it fits into a transformed media education.

Under this transformed curriculum, where do traditional areas of media education content fall? In particular, what happens to traditional practices—broadcast and cable management, broadcast journalism, media performance (announcing, newscasting, etc.), audience research, marketing analysis, broadcast production (video, radio, studio formats, sports remotes, etc.)? What is left for students to do within the media literacy–based curriculum? We have, all along, suggested a direction for practice toward the development of public sphere activity; but we need to exemplify more concretely this type of practice.

Media Institutions and Practices

Students should gain knowledge of the significance of overall patterns of media ownership and control within the context of an awareness of other important sources of power and influence the media. As students focus on institutions they will develop expertise in the determinants of national and international media practice. This can be extended into ten areas: ownership and control; media institutions; the state, the law and policy; self-regulation by the media; economic determinants; advertisers; audience construction and use; media personnel; organization of production practices; and forms of technology.

Familiar words pop up here, but there are some missing terms also—management, broadcast, new (as in technologies), marketing, public relations, and so on. These are the kinds of terms that pop up in course titles and that signal "job" to the student and "FTE" to the administration. Instead, we want to emphasize how institutional practices can be given a transformed meaning by placing them in different classroom and nonclassroom settings; and that this can occur without giving up "practice." A concrete class situation will illustrate our approach here.

Imagine a course that covers the media institutions and political economy of the U.S. media. Such a course would cover many of the elements laid out above, but how would it develop practical knowledge? First of all, in simply addressing the particular effects of law, policy and economy on media institutions, a certain level of practical problems and solutions arises. But how can we concretize this for the student (that is, create something for the student to do)? In the traditional management course, this is no problem: have them do simulations, determine ratings, chart personnel, and so on. But why not create alternative simulations that require not only these skills but also alternative ones? These same practical matters are the concerns of nonprofit groups, public media institutions, media activist and arts groups, and so on, but these organizations also provide the opportunity to question old practices and try new ones. In addition, imaginative alternative systems, with different and perhaps more democratic practices, have been proposed. Why not examine the interface of theory/practice at the experimental level? For example, students can be asked to program an alternative channel of television that assumes a different set of priorities and purposes generated by values that are central to the widening of the public sphere. Such a project would still require the design of a broadcast schedule—assessing scheduling, advertising, audience research, balancing of program types, market share, and so forth. Basic patterns of current practice would be treated but with added dimensions of evaluation and imaginative application and transformation. Thus, the practical and the hands-on can be central to a critical course, the only loss being the celebration and rote learning of entrenched models of business practice.

Media Production

It was out of our own reflections upon our experiences in teaching undergraduate media production that this book took shape. The previous chapter laid out our basic view of how production courses should be conceived: a focus on a critical view of media making as representational, ideological and political; an emphasis on process over product; a stress on ethics and social responsibility (assessing the canons of current practice and experimenting with other forms); an attention to the historical development of both production practices and equipment (giving centrality to single-camera field production).

Ultimately, our aim has been to rid media studies of the ethos that comes with the professional production model, an ethos that rigidly separates production from media study as an area of inquiry and that generates a celebratory and addictive stance toward technology. We can imagine an ideal structure in which production would become just one part of an integrated curriculum, not a separate track or series of courses.

We imagine two possibilities here: (1) production courses are remodeled to include the concerns we have outlined; (2) the elimination of production courses, per se, and instead treating production within a variety of class contexts.

In the first option, the traditional sequence of production (promising initiation into ever-advancing realms of technology) would be replaced by classes such as Media Anti-aesthetics, Documenting the Community, Video Meaning-making, Sound Sense, and so on. Such courses would center not on the act of production, but rather on the three areas of media literacy. In a transformed curriculum, production classes would require students to read and discuss such texts as *Representing Reality* (Nichols, 1991), *Visible Fictions* (Ellis, 1982) or *Television: Technology as Cultural Form* (Williams, 1975). One further point is worth noting: if production is going on within a department, then there is no reason it cannot become the site for other courses to become involved in practice, for production needs audience analysis, evaluation, management, distribution, economic study, textual analysis, and so on. In other words, why not bring to bear the supposed *theory* courses on the supposed *practical* courses?

In the second option, only one self-standing production course would exist—an introductory class called Workshop in Media Tools. This class would introduce students to the basic technology of video and audio, and would deal explicitly with the attitudinal, ethical and pedagogical dimensions of using technology. From this point on, production would take up its place in two spaces within the curriculum: within other classes and in outside, workshop experiences.

Production can and in many ways should be a part of any course in media study. Under this model, a course such as Feminism and the Media could contain elements of theoretical analysis, historical research, audience study and feminist video practice. Likewise, any course—from histories of various media to international communication—could contain projects involving the use of the tools of production. More focused and long-term production projects would take place in practicum situations where students would experiment with various media-making practices. The ideal location for this kind of workshop orientation would be within a space provided by the department for all of its students to participate in various ways in an experiment in radical democracy, that is, a public sphere.

The Public Sphere Practicum

If we take the models of democratic media systems developed by Keane (1991) and Curran (1992), we can begin to envision how the media might function in a different way as far as the public sphere is concerned. Within media education we might be able to take a step beyond simply abstract reflection on this functioning. We might, in fact, turn our resources away from such self-serving adventures as university sports coverage and local news emulation, and turn them directly toward the development of a model media system. Such an experiment would function as a small-scale simulation of a model such as Curran's. Students would participate in the formation of associations that function as public media organizations of varying kinds. In Curran's model these would include a private enterprise sector, a general purpose public service system, a civic sector (consisting of party and subcultural tiers) and an autonomous professional sector. Students would participate in setting up the system, and thus would experience and work through the problems inherent in forming genuinely radical democratic institutions.

Whatever the final practical arrangements for the experiment, it would have to provide for public dialogue from diverse perspectives; it would allow a space for students to interrogate the social conditions of the university; and it would provide assistance to various organizations in representing their viewpoints to a wider public. The result would be a publicly regulated sphere of media activity with the students acting in various positions of authority—from media producers, to organizational heads, to public representatives. This would be a direct experiment in citizenship that at the same time would provide media students with practical hands-on experience.

We could envision a miniature public sphere, where students coordinate the programming of the campus cable channel, radio station and other news outlets. Students would be responsible for airing issues of importance to diverse groups of the student body—the college political party groups, the black student caucus, the gay-lesbian alliance, the fraternity/sorority system, and so forth. This media public sphere would provide an arena where student concerns, experiences, histories, discourses and desires could be aired and contested. Such a project is not merely utopian. Such a project could easily take off if it were given the amount of resources current media departments plunk into sports vans, business- and advertising-oriented mockups, and industry tie-ins. The question is whether we in the university have the will to attempt such an ambitious experiment in democracy.

CONCLUSION

This tool kit offers some possibilities for transforming media education from its present status quo. Faculty who are in solidarity with the principles of critical pedagogy laid out here will have to work out the concrete structural and curricular forms that suit their own context. The contextual is crucial here, and we hope that our thoughts on this project will generate messages from different sites, different contexts, that will become a part of our further projects in critical media education.

Whatever the direction that our further work (and the work of others) on transforming media education takes, critical pedagogy demands that the primary emphasis of education be placed upon the renewal of the public sphere and the project of social democracy. The university must change through a process of redefinition, abandoning the protected status of "ivory tower" and entering the "real world" of social relations that construct the various cultural sites of oppression and struggle. Through a historical understanding of human political struggle, critical educators recognize the political dimensions of the classroom and work to create an environment in which the transformation of consciousness, the new formation of self, may occur. New definitions of the university, classroom, disciplines, authority, success and curriculum—new definitions of education—must emerge in the decade ahead for the goals of the new century to be realized.

NOTES

1. The university has never fully developed this function and thus, the ability of the university as an institution to stand outside of economic and state influence must be seen as an idealized utopian vision. However, actual practices within the university do allow or disallow such creative/subversive practices, and current institutional arrangements more and more work against these kinds of actions.

2. A thoroughly transformed pedagogy cannot ignore the extent to which the public sphere has functioned to shut down diversity. An openness to difference is not enough if this simply means allowing feminist, ethnic and subaltern groups a minimal space within a patriarchially constructed public sphere. Marginalized interests must actually come to be represented as public interests that are central to our educational institutions.

3. These goals are drawn from the Miami Plan for Liberal Education and are adapted to the specifics of media study. The Miami Plan's general goals are to "nurture capabilities for creatively transforming human culture, enlarge personal and vocational pathways and extend liberal learning through a lifetime" (Miami University Liberal Education Forum, 1989, 7). Thus, liberal education is aimed at how one lives, and particularly at reshaping not only the content but the form of work.

4. It is our feeling that the common core should be retained as an idea despite its problems. The core, in principle and sometimes in practice, builds a sense of community, provides coherence and direction, and furthers the development of faculty/student working relationships.

Bibliography

Alvarado, Manuel. (1990). "The Place and Purpose of Media Education." Introductory Plenary Presentation, 8 April 1990, BFI Education Easter School, Liverpool.

Apple, Michael. (1990). *Ideology and Curriculum*. New York: Routledge.

Arac, Jonathan. (1986). *Postmodernism and Politics*. Minneapolis: University of Minnesota Press.

Aronowitz, Stanley. (1981). *The Crisis in Historical Materialism*. New York: Praeger.

_____ . (1989). "Working-Class Identity and Celluloid Fantasies in the Electronic Age." In *Popular Culture, Schooling and Everyday Life*, ed. H. Giroux and R. Simon, 197–218. Granby, Mass.: Bergin & Garvey.

Aronowitz, Stanley, and Henry Giroux. (1985). *Education Under Siege*. South Hadley, Mass.: Bergin & Garvey.

_____ . (1991). *Postmodern Education*. Minneapolis: University of Minnesota Press.

Association for Education in Journalism and Mass Communication (AEJMC). (1989). "Challenges and Opportunities in Journalism and Mass Communication Education." *Journalism Educator* (Spring): A1–A24.

Baudrillard, Jean. (1988). *Selected Writings*. Stanford, Calif.: Stanford University Press.

Becker, Lee. (1989). "Enrollment Growth Exceeds National University Averages." *Journalism Educator* (Autumn): 3–15.

Ben-David, Joseph. (1972). *American Higher Education*. New York: McGraw-Hill.

Berlo, D. K. (1960). *The Process of Communication*. New York: Holt, Rinehart & Winston.

Blanchard, Robert. (1988a). "Beyond the Generic Curriculum: The Enriched Major for Journalism and Mass Communication." *Insights* (October): 9–12.

———. (1988b). "Our Emerging Role in Liberal and Media Studies." *Journalism Educator* (Autumn): 28–31.

Blanchard, Robert, and William Christ. (1988). "Professional and Liberal Education: An Agenda for Journalism and Mass Communication." *ACA Bulletin* (April): 3–8.

Bloom, Allan. (1987). *The Closing of the American Mind.* New York: Simon and Schuster.

Blumer, Jay, and Elihu Katz, eds. (1974). *The Uses of Mass Communication.* Beverly Hills, Calif.: Sage.

Bohn, Thomas. (1988). "Professional and Liberal Education." *ACA Bulletin* (April): 16–22.

Bowles, Samuel, and Herbert Gintis. (1976). *Schooling in Capitalist America.* New York: Basic Books.

Carey, James. (1978). "A Plea for the University Tradition." *Journalism Quarterly* 55(4): 847–855.

Carroll, Ray. (1987). "No 'Middle Ground': Professional Broadcast Education Is Liberal Education." *Feedback* (Spring): 7–10.

Corrigan, Philip. (1989). "Playing . . . Contradictions, Empowerment, and Embodiment: Punk, Pedagogy, and Popular Cultural Forms (On Ethnography and Education)." In *Popular Culture, Schooling and Everyday Life*, ed. H. Giroux and R. Simon, 67–90. Granby, Mass.: Bergin & Garvey.

Curran, James. (1992). "Mass Media and Democracy: A Reappraisal." In *Mass Media and Society*, ed. J. Curran and M. Gurevitch, 82–117. London: Edward Arnold.

Daly, J. A., G. W. Friedrich, and A. L. Vangelisti, eds. (1990). *Teaching Communication: Theory, Research and Methods.* Hillsdale, N.J.: Lawrence Erlbaum Associates.

Delia, Jesse. (1987). "Communication Research: A History." In *Handbook of Communication Science*, ed. C. R. Berger and S. Chaffee, 20–98. Newbury Park, Calif.: Sage.

Dennis, Everett. (1984). *A Report on the Future of Mass Communication Education.* Eugene: School of Journalism, University of Oregon.

Denski, Stan. (1991). "Critical Pedagogy and Media Production." *Journal of Film and Video* 43(3): 3–18.

Dewey, John. (1927). *The Public and Its Problems.* Chicago: Swallow Press.

Eagleton, Terry. (1991). *Ideology: An Introduction.* London: Verso.

Ellis, John. (1982). *Visible Fictions.* London: Routledge.

Ellsworth, Elizabeth. (1989). "Educational Media, Ideology, and the Presentation of Knowledge Through Popular Cultural Forms." In *Popular Culture, Schooling and Everyday Life*, ed. H. Giroux and R. Simon, 47–66. Grandby, Mass.: Bergin & Garvey.

Engel, Michael. (1991). "Ideology and the Politics of Public Higher Education: Responses to Budget Crisis and Curricular Reorganization." In *The Liberal Arts in a Time of Crisis*, ed. B. A. Scott, 33–46. New York: Praeger.

Felski, Rita. (1989). *Beyond Feminist Aesthetics*. Cambridge, Mass.: Harvard University Press.

Fine, Michelle. (1989). "Silencing and Nurturing Voice in an Improbable Context: Urban Adolescents in Public School." In *Critical Pedagogy, the State, and Cultural Struggle*, ed. H. Giroux and P. McLaren, 152–173. Albany: SUNY.

Foucault, Michel. (1972). "The Discourse on Language." In *The Archaeology of Knowledge*. London: Tavistock.

———. (1977). *Language, Counter-memory, Practice: Selected Essays and Interviews*, ed. D. Bouchard. Ithaca: Cornell University Press.

———. (1979). *Discipline and Punish*. New York: Vintage.

———. (1988). *Politics, Philosophy, Culture: Interviews and Other Writings, 1977–1984*, ed. L. Kritzman. New York: Routledge.

———. (1989). *Foucault Live*, ed. S. Lotringer, New York: Semiotext(e).

Fraser, Nancy. (1990). "Rethinking the Public Sphere: A Contribution to the Critique of Actually Existing Democracy." *Social Text* 25(26): 56–80.

Freire, Paulo. (1989). *Pedagogy of the Oppressed*. New York: Continuum.

Freire, Paulo, and Donaldo Macedo. (1987). *Literacy: Reading the Word & the World*. Granby, Mass.: Bergin & Garvey.

Giroux, Henry. (1988). *Schooling and the Struggle for Public Life*. Minneapolis: University of Minnesota Press.

———. (1990). "Liberal Arts Education and the Struggle for Public Life: Dreaming about Democracy." *South Atlantic Quarterly* 89(1): 113–138.

———. (1992). *Border Crossings*. New York: Routledge.

Giroux, Henry, ed. (1991). *Postmodernism, Feminism, and Cultural Politics*. Albany: SUNY.

Giroux, Henry, and Peter McLaren, eds. (1989). *Critical Pedagogy, the State, and Cultural Struggle*. Albany: SUNY.

Giroux, Henry, and Roger Simon, eds. (1989). *Popular Culture, Schooling and Everyday Life*. Granby, Mass.: Bergin & Garvey.

Gitlin, Todd. (1978). "Media Sociology: The Dominant Paradigm." *Theory and Society* 6: 205–253.

———. (1980). *The Whole World Is Watching*. Berkeley: University of California Press.

Gless, Darryl, and Barbara Herrnstein Smith. (1992). *The Politics of the Liberal Arts*. Durham, N.C.: Duke University Press.

"The Governor's Response, Feb. 26, 1992." (1992). *Miami University Report* 11(30): 4.

Graff, Gerald. (1985). *Criticism in the University*. Evanston, Ill.: Northwestern University Press.

_____ . (1988). "Foreword." In *Universities and the Myth of Cultural Decline*, ed. J. Herron, 9–19. Detroit: Wayne State University Press.

_____ . (1992). "Teach the Conflicts." In *The Politics of the Liberal Arts*, ed. D. Gless and B. Smith, 57–74. Durham: Duke University Press.

Gramsci, Antonio. (1971). *Selections From Prison Notebooks*, ed. and trans. Q. Honre and G. Smith. New York: International Press.

Grossberg, Lawrence. (1989). "Pedagogy in the Present: Politics, Postmodernity and the Popular." In *Popular Culture, Schooling and Everyday Life*, ed. H. Giroux and R. Simon, 91–116. Granby, Mass.: Bergin & Garvey.

_____ . (1992). *We Gotta Get Out of This Place*. New York and London: Routledge.

Gurevitch, Michael, Tony Bennett, James Curran and Janet Woollacott. (1982). *Culture, Society and the Media*. London: Methuen.

Hall, Stuart. (1980). "Cultural Studies: Two Paradigms." *Media, Culture and Society* 2: 57–72.

_____ . (1990). "The Emergence of Cultural Studies and the Crisis of the Humanities." *October* 53: 11–24.

Harvey, David. (1982). *The Limits to Capital*. Chicago: University of Chicago Press.

Hazinski, David. (1989). "Equal Time." *Feedback* (Winter): 16–24.

Heath, Stephen. (1990). "Representing Television." In *Logics of Television*, ed. P. Mellencamp, 267–302. Bloomington: Indiana University Press.

Hebdige, Dick. (1988). *Hiding in the Light*. New York: Routledge.

Held, David. (1987). *Models of Democracy*. Stanford, Calif.: Stanford University Press.

Herron, Jerry. (1988). *Universities and the Myth of Cultural Decline*. Detroit: Wayne State University Press.

Hirsch, E. D. (1987). *Cultural Literacy: What Every American Needs to Know*. Boston: Houghton Mifflin.

Journal of Communication. (1983). Vol. 33, no. 3: "Ferment in the Field."

Katz, Elihu, Jay Blumer, and Michael Gurevitch. (1974). "Utilization of Mass Communication by the Individual." In *The Uses of Mass Communication*, ed. J. Blumer and E. Katz, 19–34. Beverly Hills, Calif.: Sage.

Katzen, May. (1975). *Mass Communication: Teaching and Studies at Universities*. Paris: Unesco Press.

Keane, John. (1991). *The Media and Democracy*. Cambridge, England: Polity Press.

Kitross, John. (1989). "Six Decades of Education for Broadcasting . . . and Counting." *Feedback* (Fall): 30–42.

Klapper, Joseph. (1960). *The Effects of Mass Communication*. New York: Free Press.

Kroker, Arthur, and David Cook. (1988). *The Postmodern Scene*. New York: St. Martin's Press.

Limberg, Val. (1987). "Administrative Structures and Program Orientation in Broadcast Communications Curriculum. *Feedback* (Summer): 22–28.

Lippmann, Walter. (1921). *Public Opinion*. New York: Macmillan.

Lusted, David. (1986). "Why pedagogy?" *Screen* 29(5): 2–15.

Lyotard, Jean-François. (1984). *The Postmodern Condition: A Report on Knowledge*. Minneapolis: University of Minnesota Press.

McCain, Thomas A. (1990). "Teaching Mass Communication and Telecommunication." In *Teaching Communication: Theory, Research and Methods*, eds. J. A. Daly, G. W. Friedrich, and A. L. Vangelisti. Hillsdale, N.J.: Lawrence Erlbaum Associates.

McClary, Susan. (1989/90). "This Is Not a Story My People Tell: Musical Time and Space According to Laurie Anderson." *Discourse* 12(1): 104–128.

McLaren, Peter. (1988). "Foreword: Critical Theory and the Meaning of Hope." In *Teachers as Intellectuals,* ed. H. Giroux, ix–xxi. Granby, Mass.: Bergin & Garvey.

———. (1989). *Life in Schools*. New York: Longman.

———. (1992). "Critical Pedagogy, Postcolonial Politics and Redemptive Remembrance." In *Learner Factors/Teacher Factors: Issues in Literacy and Instruction* (Fortieth Yearbook, National Reading Conference), 31–48. Chicago: National Reading Conference, Inc.

McQuail, Dennis. (1984). *Mass Communication Theory: An Introduction*. Newbury Park, Calif.: Sage.

Merton, Robert. (1957/67). *Social Theory and Social Structure*. Glencoe, Ill.: Free Press.

Miami University Liberal Education Forum. (1989). *The Miami Plan for Liberal Education*. Oxford, Ohio: Miami University.

Minnich, Elizabeth Kamarck. (1990). *Transforming Knowledge*. Philadelphia: Temple University Press.

———. (1992). "From Ivory Tower to Tower of Babel?" In *The Politics of the Liberal Arts*, ed. D. Gless and B. Smith, 187–200. Durham, N.C.: Duke University Press.

Morris, Meaghan. (1988). "Banality in Cultural Studies." *Discourse* 10(2): 3–29.

Nelson, Cary. (1985). "Poststructuralism and Communication." *Journal of Communication Inquiry* 9(2).

Nichols, Bill. (1981). *Ideology and the Image*. Bloomington: Indiana University Press.

———. (1983). "The Voice of Documentary." *Film Quarterly* 36(3): 17–30.

———. (1991). *Representing Reality: Issues and Concepts in Documentary*. Bloomington: Indiana University Press.

Oakley, Francis. (1992). "Against Nostalgia: Reflections on Our Present Discontents in American Higher Education." In *The Politics of the Liberal Arts*, ed. D. Gless and B. Smith, 267–290. Durham, N.C.: Duke University Press.

Oestereicher, Emil. (1991). "The Depoliticization of the Liberal Arts." In *The Liberal Arts in a Time of Crisis*, ed. B. A. Scott, 11–16. New York: Praeger.

Palmgreen, Phillip. Lawrence Wenner, and Karl Rosengren. (1985). "Uses and Gratifications Research: The Past Ten Years." In *Media Gratifications Research: Current Perspectives*, ed. K. Rosengren, L. Wenner, and P. Palmgreen, 11–37. Beverly Hills, Calif.: Sage.

Peters, John. (1988). "The Need for Theoretical Foundations: Reply to Gonzalez." *Communication Research* 15(3): 309–317.

Pratt, Mary Louise. (1990). "Humanities for the Future: Reflections on the Western Culture Debate at Stanford." *South Atlantic Quarterly* 89(1): 7–25.

Renz, Byron. (1987). "Tracking in Curriculum: An Interdisciplinary Approach. *Feedback* (Winter): 31–39.

Said, Edward W. (1983). *The World, the Text and the Critic*. Cambridge: Harvard University Press.

Scott, Barbara Ann. (1983). *Crisis Management in American Higher Education*. New York: Praeger.

———. (1991). *The Liberal Arts in a Time of Crisis*. New York: Praeger.

Severn, Werner, and James Tankard. (1992). *Communication Theories: Origins, Methods, and Uses in the Mass Media*. New York: Longman.

Sholle, David. (1988). "Critical Studies: From the Theory of Ideology to Power/Knowledge." *Critical Studies in Mass Communication* 5(1): 16–41.

———. (1991). "Resistance: Pinning Down a Wandering Concept in Cultural Studies Discourse." *Journal of Urban and Cultural Studies* 11(1): 87–106.

Shor, Ira, and Paulo Freire. (1987). *A Pedagogy for Liberation*. Granby, Mass.: Bergin & Garvey.

Smith, Barbara Herrnstein. (1992). "Introduction: The Public, the Press and the Professors." In *The Politics of the Liberal Arts*, ed. D. Gless and B. Smith, 1–12. Durham, N.C.: Duke University Press.

Sykes, Charles T. (1990). *ProfScam: Professors and the Demise of Higher Education*. New York: St. Martin's Press.

Ulmer, Gregory. (1989). *Teletheory: Grammatology in the Age of Video*. New York: Routledge.

Warner, Charles, and Yu-Mei Liu. (1990). "Broadcast Curriculum Profile." *Feedback* (Summer): 6–7.

Wexler, Philip. (1989). "Curriculum in the Closed Society." In *Critical Pedagogy, the State, and Cultural Struggle*, ed. H. Giroux and P. McLaren, 92–104. Albany: SUNY.

Williams, Raymond. (1975). *Television: Technology as Cultural Form*. New York: Schocken Books.

———. (1989). *Resources of Hope*. New York: Verso.

Index

About the Authors

DAVID SHOLLE is Assistant Professor of Communication at Miami University in Ohio.

STAN DENSKI is Assistant Professor in the Department of Communication and Theatre at Indiana University.

Both have co-authored chapters in *Critical Literacy* (Lankshear and McLaren, editors, 1993) and *Mediated Men: Images of Males in Mass Media* (Craig, editor, 1991).